The
Digestive
System

Titles in the Understanding the Human Body series include:

Understanding
THE HUMAN BODY

The Digestive System

Pam Walker and Elaine Wood

LUCENT BOOKS®

THOMSON
™
GALE

San Diego • Detroit • New York • San Francisco • Cleveland • New Haven, Conn. • Waterville, Maine • London • Munich

THOMSON

━━━━━✦━━━━━ ™

GALE

© 2003 by Lucent Books. Lucent Books is an imprint of The Gale Group, Inc.,
a division of Thomson Learning, Inc.

Lucent Books® and Thomson Learning™ are trademarks used herein under license.

For more information, contact
Lucent Books
27500 Drake Rd.
Farmington Hills, MI 48331-3535
Or you can visit our Internet site at http://www.gale.com

LIBRARY OF CONGRESS CATALOGING-IN-PUBLICATION DATA

Walker, Pam, 1958–
  The Digestive System / by Pam Walker and Elaine Wood.
    p. cm. — (Understanding the human body)
Includes bibliographical references and index.
Summary: Discusses the organs and function of the human digestive system, the
nutrients essential for good health, how nutrients are processed by the body, and
the medical treatments available for digestive disorders.
  ISBN 1-59018-150-6
  1. Digestive organs—Juvenile literature. [1. Digestive system. 2. Digestion. 3.
Nutrition.] I. Wood, Elaine, 1950– II. Title. III. Series.
  QP145 .W25 2002
  612.3—dc21
 	
2001006246

Printed in the United States of America

CONTENTS

FOREWORD

Since Earth first formed, countless creatures have come and gone. Dinosaurs and other types of land and sea animals all fell prey to climatic shifts, food shortages, and myriad other environmental factors. However, one species—human beings—survived throughout tens of thousands of years of evolution, adjusting to changes in climate and moving when food was scarce. The primary reason human beings were able to do this is that they possess a complex and adaptable brain and body.

The human body is comprised of organs, tissue, and bone that work independently and together to sustain life. Although it is both remarkable and unique, the human body shares features with other living organisms: the need to eat, breathe, and eliminate waste; the need to reproduce and eventually die.

Human beings, however, have many characteristics that other living creatures do not. The adaptable brain is responsible for these characteristics. Human beings, for example, have excellent memories; they can recall events that took place twenty, thirty, even fifty years earlier. Human beings also possess a high level of intelligence. Their unique capacity to invent, create, and innovate has led to discoveries and inventions such as vaccines, automobiles, and computers. And the human brain allows people to feel and respond to a variety of emotions. No other creature on Earth has such a broad range of abilities.

Although the human brain physically resembles a large, soft walnut, its capabilities seem limitless. The brain controls the body's movement, enabling humans to sprint, jog, walk, and crawl. It controls the body's internal functions, allowing people to breathe and maintain a heartbeat without effort. And it controls a person's creative talent, giving him or her the ability to write novels, paint masterpieces, or compose music.

Like a computer, the brain runs a network of body systems that keep human beings alive. The nervous system relays the brain's messages to the rest of the body. The respiratory system draws in life-sustaining oxygen and expels carbon dioxide waste. The circulatory system carries that oxygen to and from the body's vital organs. The reproductive system allows humans to continue their species and flourish as the dominant creatures on the planet. The digestive system takes in vital nutrients and converts them into the energy the body needs to grow. And the immune system protects the body from disease and foreign objects. When all of these systems work properly, the result is an intricate, extraordinary living machine.

Even when some of the systems are not working properly, the human body can often adapt. Healthy people have two kidneys, but, if necessary, they can live with just one. Doctors can remove a defective liver, heart, lung, or pancreas and replace it with a working one from another body. And a person blinded by an accident, disease, or birth defect can live a perfectly normal life by developing other senses to make up for the loss of sight.

The human body adapts to countless external factors as well. It sweats to cool off, adjusts the level of oxygen it needs at high altitudes, and derives nutritional value from a wide variety of foods, making do with what is available in a given region.

Only under tremendous duress does the human body cease to function. Extreme fluctuations in temperature, an invasion by hardy germs, or severe physical damage can halt normal bodily functions and cause death. Yet, even in such circumstances, the body continues to try to repair itself. The body of a diabetic, for example, will take in extra liquid and try to expel excess glucose through the urine. And a body exposed to extremely low temperatures will shiver in an effort to generate its own heat.

Lucent's Understanding the Human Body series explores different systems of the human body. Each volume describes the parts of a given body system and how they work both individually and collectively. Unique characteristics, malfunctions, and cutting edge medical procedures and technologies are also discussed. Photographs, diagrams, and glossaries enhance the text, and annotated bibliographies provide readers with opportunities for further discussion and research.

A Journey down the Food Tube

All living things require energy. Energy fuels life processes such as growth, movement, and reproduction. Food provides humans and other living things with energy and the raw materials necessary for building new cells. Food is not a simple substance; it is a mixture of chemicals and nutrients. This mixture is too complex to be delivered straight to the cells. Cells cannot directly absorb the nutrients locked in food. Therefore, each morsel of food taken into the body is changed to a form that can be absorbed by cells.

The digestive system is the place where these changes in food occur. The digestive system can be compared to a factory that dismantles food. It is within this huge food processor that complex food is broken down into a simple, usable form. The end products of food digestion are simple, basic nutrients.

The process of digestion has many stages. During the process, food is altered in two ways: physically by chewing and churning, and chemically by enzyme action. Enzymes are special proteins that break the bonds that hold food molecules together. As soon as food is placed in the mouth, chemical and physical digestion begins.

During digestion, food travels through a long, muscular food tube called the alimentary canal or the gastrointestinal (GI) tract. After digestion, usable food is absorbed by the body. The undigested portions of food are expelled in the form of feces through the anus. About three gallons of digested food, liquids, and digestive juices flow through the GI tract daily. A little more than 0.2 pints of this material is lost as waste.

Parts of the Food Tube

The human digestive system is composed of the alimentary canal and its accessory organs. The accessory organs are located along the length of the tube. The food tube itself consists of the mouth, pharynx, esophagus, stomach, small intestine, large intestine, and anus. The tube's length is difficult to estimate because it contracts and expands while digestion is in progress. An inactive food tube

The food we eat nourishes our bodies by providing energy and the materials necessary for building new cells.

measures more than nine yards in length, while the active version is about five-and-a-half yards long.

The accessory organs of the digestive system include the teeth, tongue, salivary glands, pancreas, liver, and gallbladder. Each part of the digestive system makes a vital contribution to the breakdown of food. In addition, other organs, such as those in the nervous and circulatory systems, also play important roles in digestion. During a person's lifetime, the food tube and its supporting components may process 60,000 to 100,000 pounds of food.

The Beginning of the Journey

Food enters the human digestive system through the mouth, or oral cavity. Lips form the entrance to the mouth. Externally, lips are covered with skin. Internally, they are coated by mucous membrane, like the entire oral cavity. Cheeks are continuous with the lips and form the sides of the mouth. A large muscle lies between the outer skin of the cheeks and the inner mucous lining. The roof of the mouth is composed of the hard and soft palates, which are made of bone, blood vessels, muscle fibers, and nerves.

Anchored to the floor of the oral cavity is the tongue. Because it is made up of muscle fibers, the tongue is able to move in various directions. During the process of chewing, the tongue helps mix food with saliva and place it between the teeth. The tongue's surface is covered with rough elevations called papillae, some of which contain taste buds. In fact, there are about nine thousand taste buds on the tongue. Taste buds allow a person to experience the flavors of food: sweet, sour, salty, or bitter. They are also sensitive to cold, heat, and pressure.

In the mouth, food is changed to a solution. This solution enters trenchlike depressions surrounding the papillae. Here, it makes contact with the taste buds. As the solution enters the openings of the taste buds, it stimulates nerve endings in the taste cells. Nerve fibers located at the base of the taste buds transport these impulses to the brain.

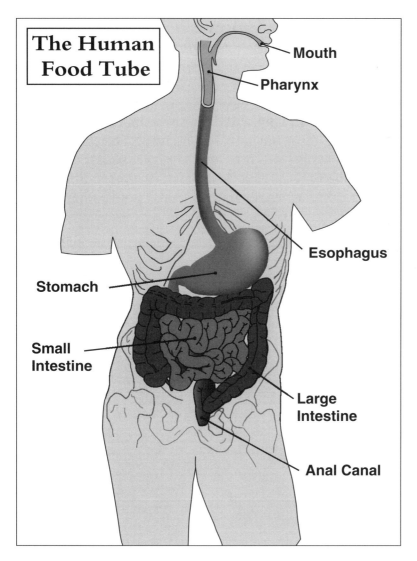

The Human Food Tube

Mouth

Pharynx

Esophagus

Stomach

Small Intestine

Large Intestine

Anal Canal

The floor and underside of the tongue have numerous blood vessels. Under the tongue, the large vein and many smaller vessels can be seen shining through the tongue's mucous membrane. These vessels lie very close to the surface. The close proximity of the blood vessels to the tongue's surface can be beneficial to patients taking certain types of medicine. People who need medicines delivered quickly to the bloodstream are sometimes instructed to place the pills or tablets under their tongues.

Mechanical Breakdown

Teeth are located in the upper and lower jaws at the front and sides of the oral cavity. Their job is to tear and grind food. The specific function of each tooth is determined by its shape. Adults generally have thirty-two permanent teeth, sixteen in each jaw. These include four pairs of chisel-shaped front teeth called incisors. The sharp edges of incisors are used to bite into large pieces of food. Four cone-shaped teeth, called cuspids or canines, grasp and tear food. Eight premolars and twelve molars have flattened surfaces for grinding. Grinding food increases its

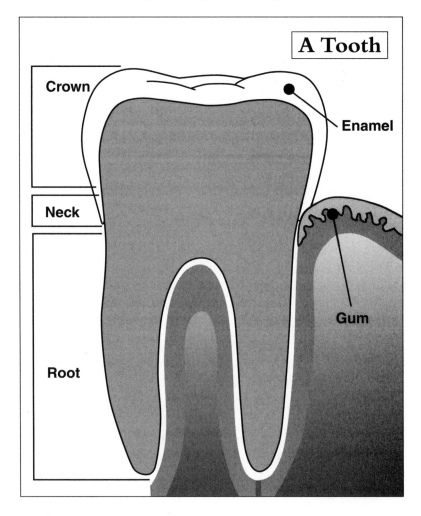

surface area and allows digestive enzymes to react more effectively with the food molecules.

Each tooth has three basic parts: crown, neck, and root. The crown is the exposed portion of a tooth. It is the part of the tooth seen above the gum line. Enamel, the hardest and chemically most stable substance in the body, covers the crown. Enamel protects a tooth from decay. If it is damaged by abrasive action, enamel is not replaced. The neck of the tooth is the narrow part that joins the crown to the root. The root may be single or have two or more projections. It fits into a socket in the upper or lower jaw. A tooth is not cemented into its socket; it is held there by relatively soft gum tissue.

The Importance of Oral Secretions

As food is chewed, it is softened and lubricated by oral secretions called saliva. Saliva flows into the mouth when nerve endings in the mouth are stimulated. Hunger, smell, emotional upset, and objects in the mouth are some of the stimuli that prompt the secretion of saliva. The average adult produces 2.1 to 3.6 pints of saliva every twenty-four hours.

Three pairs of salivary glands produce and secrete saliva into the mouth. The largest of these are the pyramid-shaped parotid glands. The parotid glands are found under the skin, in front of and below the ear. These are the glands that become inflamed during an attack of the mumps. The parotid glands produce saliva of watery consistency that contains the enzyme amylase. Amylase begins the breakdown of starch in food. Amylase is just one of the more than seven hundred enzymes produced by the human body. Enzymes speed up chemical reactions.

Below the parotid glands are the submandibular glands. They are called mixed or compound glands because they make both enzymes and mucus. The submandibulars are found in the floor of the mouth on the inside surface of the lower jaw. The smallest salivary glands are the sublingual glands, which are found under mucous membranes covering the floor of the mouth under the tongue. Their cells primarily produce thick mucus.

The action of the tongue, teeth, and saliva turns food in the mouth into a soft mass called a bolus. Once a food bolus leaves the mouth, it passes into a region at the back of the throat called the pharynx. The pharynx is a common passageway for food and air. A flap of tissue, the uvula, extends from the soft palate into the opening of the pharynx. When swallowing occurs, the uvula blocks food from entering the nasal cavity region. As an added precaution, nerve impulses halt breathing as a bolus is swallowed. This keeps food out of the respiratory tract. The bolus then enters the muscular tube at the back of the pharynx called the esophagus or gullet.

The Muscular Tube

The act of swallowing begins as a voluntary process but becomes involuntary once food reaches the smooth muscles of the esophagus. An adult's esophagus is a collapsible tube about ten inches long. It protrudes through the diaphragm and ends at the opening of the stomach. Food does not free-fall down the esophagus. It is moved along by muscles that contract and relax in a process called peristalsis. These muscle movements press and squeeze food along the tube. Since swallowing does not depend on gravity, the process of peristalsis explains why people can swallow while standing on their head or why astronauts in outer space can swallow food. The passage of food along this muscular tube takes from five to nine seconds. When the peristaltic waves reach the stomach, muscles that guard the opening to the stomach relax. As a result, the bolus passes into the stomach.

The Temporary Storage Tank

The stomach, located between the ribs and above the waist, is a pouchlike cavity about 9.8 inches long. Its diameter depends on how much food it contains. Men's stomachs are larger than those of women. At maximum capacity, the average stomach can hold approximately one gallon of food. When it is empty, it collapses in on itself and is about the size of a large sausage. The upper section of the stomach is called the fundus. The fundus is sepa-

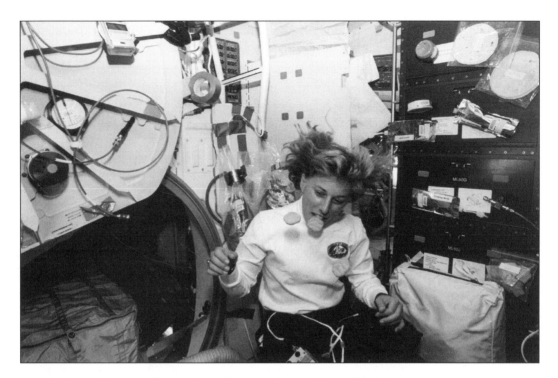

rated from the esophagus by a layer of muscles called the cardiac sphincter. This circular layer of muscles, so named because it is near the heart, acts as a valve that lets food into the stomach.

From the fundus, food travels to the middle section, or body, of the stomach. Eventually, food passes to the lower portion of the stomach, the pylorus. Another layer of muscles called the pyloric sphincter regulates the passage of food from the stomach to the upper portion of the small intestine. After a person eats, about 3.2 pints of food remain in the stomach for two to six hours. Generally, it takes four hours for the stomach to empty after eating a well-balanced meal. However, emptying may take up to six hours if the meal is high in fat content.

Most people think of the stomach as the main digestive organ, but it is not. The stomach is really an acid bath and a temporary storage tank for food. The contents of the stomach maintain a pH of 1.5 to 2.5. (The pH measures the hydrogen-ion concentration.) This is a very acidic condition. In fact, the

Astronauts can swallow food in the weightlessness of space because of the muscular contractions of the esophagus.

materials in the stomach are 3 million times more acidic than those in the bloodstream.

The stomach is made of three layers of muscles coated on the interior with a mucous lining. It is the mucous lining of the stomach that prevents the acid from eating into the stomach wall. The very acidic conditions of the gastric juices wear away the mucous coating over time. In order to maintain a healthy stomach lining, new mucus-producing cells must be continuously made to replace damaged ones.

In the stomach, mechanical digestion continues as these muscles push and churn food into smaller fragments. Chemical digestion in the stomach is triggered by different stimuli. The sight, smell, and taste of food cause the stomach to release gastric juices. In these juices are protein-digesting enzymes, mucus, and hydrochloric acid.

A hormone called gastrin helps regulate the acidity, or pH, of the stomach. Gastrin is produced when the acidity in the stomach nears 2.5. The release of gastrin causes the production of additional hydrochloric acid to lower the acidity of the stomach to a pH of 1.5. However, if the pH of the stomach becomes too acidic (lower than 1.5), gastrin blocks further release of hydrochloric acid. This is important because if digested liquid entering the small intestine is too acidic, it cannot be neutralized.

The Body's Main Digestive Organ

After being processed by the stomach, food looks like heavy cream. This material, called chyme, leaves the stomach through the pyloric sphincter. It then enters the upper portion of the small intestine, an area called the duodenum. Only a few spoonfuls of chyme are squirted through the pyloric sphincter every few minutes. Each portion of the acidic chyme is neutralized in the duodenum before more chyme is added.

The small intestine is the body's main digestive organ. When chyme enters this organ, the digestion of starches and proteins has only begun. No digestion of fats has taken place at this point. Once the food is in the small intestine, the chemical digestion of proteins, fats, and carbohydrates is completed, as chyme makes a four- to eight-hour trip through this organ. Chyme is continuously pushed along the small intestine by the squeezing and relaxing motion of peristalsis.

Located in the lower abdomen, the small intestine is a twisted passageway of coils that winds around itself. The wrapping and looping of this long tube fills most of a person's abdominal cavity. The small intestine has a diameter of about one inch. If it were stretched out, it would measure about twenty feet long. Amazingly, its total surface area exceeds 3,228 square feet. This is an area equal to the size of a large swimming pool or a tennis court.

The small intestine has three main divisions: the duodenum, the jejunum, and the ileum. The duodenum, the uppermost division, is attached to the pyloric sphincter of the stomach. It is a C-shaped structure, about 9.8 inches long, that curves around the head of the pancreas. The jejunum is about 8 feet long and connects the duodenum to the lower section of the small intestine, the ileum. The ileum, about 12 feet in length, joins the large intestine at a layer of muscles called a valve.

Accessory Digestive Organs

It is in the small intestine that most of the chemical digestion of chyme takes place. Several glands contribute their contents to aid in this digestion. The walls of the small intestine contain thousands of glands that produce intestinal juice. Cells that line the wall of the small intestine release hormones that travel to the pancreas, liver, and gallbladder.

One of these hormones causes the pancreas to release pancreatic juices. The pancreas is a pink, triangular-shaped organ located beneath the stomach. Its jobs include making digestive enzymes and regulating the balance of blood glucose in the body. The pancreas is attached to the small intestine by a duct. Through this duct, enzymes in the pancreatic juices are transported to the small intestine. Pancreatic juices aid in protein and starch digestion and begin the digestion of fat. These juices also contain a rich supply of bicarbonate, which changes the acidic chyme from the stomach into a basic or alkaline mixture. Digestive functions in the small intestine require alkaline conditions.

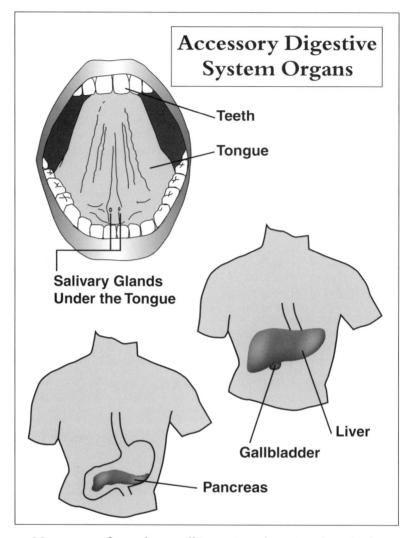

Accessory Digestive System Organs

Teeth

Tongue

Salivary Glands
Under the Tongue

Liver

Gallbladder

Pancreas

    Hormones from the small intestine also stimulate the liver to increase its output of bile. At the same time, they prod the gallbladder to release its stored bile into the common bile duct. Bile is not an enzyme and does not chemically digest fat. Instead, it acts like a detergent to emulsify or mechanically break fat into thousands of tiny particles, increasing its surface area. Bile emulsifies fat in the watery contents of the intestine much like detergent breaks down grease from a frying pan. Pancreatic enzymes are more chemically effective on small pieces of fat than on large ones.

The four-lobed, reddish-brown liver is the largest organ in the human body. The liver is about the size of a football and weighs three pounds. It is located in the upper right and central portions of the abdominal cavity, just below the diaphragm. Production of bile is just one of the liver's vital jobs in the body. The liver also makes complex carbohydrates, builds proteins, stores vitamins and minerals, produces bile salts, monitors cholesterol, and detoxifies alcohol and other poisons.

When fats are present in the small intestine, hormones travel to the liver and signal it to release bile into the duodenum through the common bile duct. As the liver continues to produce bile, excess amounts are stored in a small green sac called the gallbladder. This organ, located just beneath the liver, is three to nine inches long and can hold up to one-tenth of a pint of fluid. Bile is stored in the gallbladder until fatty food once again enters the small intestine. When this happens, hormones from the small intestine prompt the gallbladder to contract and spurt stored bile through the common bile duct into the duodenum.

Villi in the Small Intestine

Even after the digestion of fats, carbohydrates, and proteins is completed in the small intestine, the work of this organ is not finished. The combined action of intestinal juice, bile, and pancreatic juice finishes the breakdown of chyme into simple nutrients. But these nutrients must be absorbed following digestion to be of benefit to the body's cells. Absorption is aided by the unique internal shape of the small intestine. Instead of being smooth, the small intestine's internal walls are covered with millions of tiny projections called villi.

Each microscopic villus contains a network of blood and lymph vessels. These structures protruding into the intestinal space greatly increase the surface area of the small intestine. Specialized cells in the villi produce digestive enzymes. Located between the enzyme cells are goblet cells. These make mucus to lubricate the small intestine.

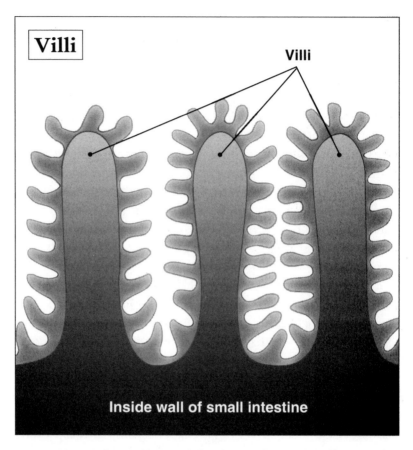

Villi

Villi

Inside wall of small intestine

Nutrients from digested food pass through villi into the bloodstream. Blood carries these nutrients to the liver. From here, the circulatory system delivers them to the heart, the pump that sends blood throughout the body. Nutrients in the blood are then delivered to cells, which use them for energy, repair, and reproduction.

The Fate of Undigested Food

Not all food that passes through the alimentary canal is digested into nutrients. Undigested food does not pass into the villi of the small intestine. Instead, it leaves the small intestine through a valve and travels into the large intestine. The large intestine is given its name because it has a greater diameter than the small intestine. At about five feet long and two-and-a-half inches wide, the large intestine extends from the valve at the small intestine to the anus. The large intestine frames the small intestine on three sides and consists of these subdivisions: cecum, appendix, colon, rectum, and anus.

The cecum, the first part of the large intestine, is shaped like a small sac. It is located in the lower right quadrant of the abdomen. A finger-shaped appendix hangs down from the cecum. Although the appendix has no digestive function in humans, it does serve to digest cellulose in some plant-eating animals, such as rabbits. Moving up the right side of the large intestine from the cecum is the ascending colon. It joins the transverse colon, which makes a turn across the abdominal cavity. On the left side of the abdomen, it turns sharply downward and is referred to as the descending colon. The descending colon runs down the left side of the abdomen and joins the S-shaped region called the sigmoid colon.

The duties of the large intestine can be compared to a trash compactor. Its main functions are to absorb water from undigested food residues and then eliminate these residues from the body as feces. A plant material called cellulose is an example of food that cannot be digested and used by the body. Cellulose is a fiber, and it provides good bulk for feces formation. Cellulose and other undigested food spend twelve to twenty-four hours in the large intestine awaiting removal through defecation. During this wait, bacteria that live in the large intestine break down any remaining nutrients to make vitamin K. Vitamin-producing bacteria first take up residence in a person's body just a few hours after birth. They remain through life. Since undigested material in the large intestine contains very few nutrients, the only absorption that occurs from this organ consists of vitamin K, some ions, and the remaining water.

The large intestine is not lined with villi because most absorption occurs in the small intestine. However, the large intestine does contain numerous goblet cells to produce mucus. The mucus acts as a lubricant to ease the passage of undigested food to the end of the digestive tract. Eventually, the muscles of the large intestine deliver feces to the rectum.

The last seven to eight inches of the gastrointestinal tube is the rectum. The rectum empties into an external opening called the anus. The removal of feces from the rectum occurs through two rings of muscles called anal sphincters. Both of these muscles remain contracted to close the anal opening until defecation occurs.

Wrapping Up the Journey

The transformation of food into nutrients by the digestive system is truly amazing. The digestive tract is essentially a long tube that begins at the mouth and ends at the anus. Food entering this tube is not in a form that the body can use. The job of the tube and its associated organs is to convert food into simple nutritional building blocks. To be ef-

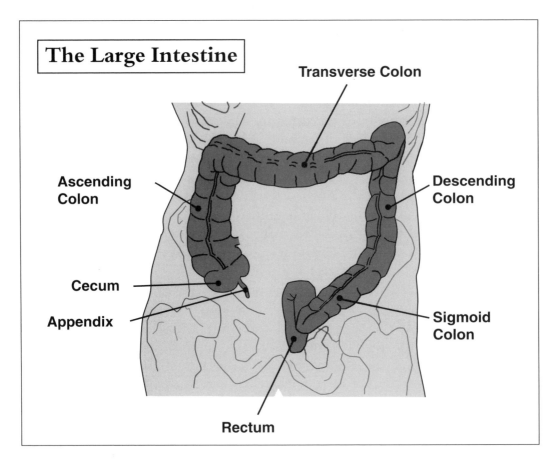

The Large Intestine

Transverse Colon

Ascending Colon

Descending Colon

Cecum

Appendix

Sigmoid Colon

Rectum

fective, the parts of this system must function in synchrony like the individual instruments in a large orchestra.

Although all components of the digestive system are important, the most exciting work takes place in the small intestine. This is where most digestion occurs, and where food begins its trip to the cells. Up to this point food has been mechanically broken apart and exposed to a few digestive chemicals. But it's in the small intestine that most chemical digestion occurs. Specialized digestive chemicals from the liver, pancreas, and lining of the small intestine meet food in this common mixing area.

Simply by responding to feelings of hunger, people unconsciously supply their bodies with basic nutrients. From these building blocks, the body makes energy, assembles new structures, and repairs old ones. Good nutrition can optimize these processes so that all body systems can function at their best.

2 | Energy for the Body

Food is essential to life. It supplies a complex blend of nutrients that support every body function. Nutrients are chemical substances that provide nourishment. The body absorbs the nutrients in food and uses them for growth, development, and maintenance. Very little of what is eaten goes to waste. More than 95 percent of the food taken into the body is used for energy.

Nutrients can be classified into two major types: macronutrients and micronutrients. Macronutrients include carbohydrates, fats, proteins, and seven minerals needed every day in large amounts. Macronutrients make up the bulk of the diet. They supply the energy and building blocks to run the body. Micronutrients are required in very small amounts. They include vitamins and fifteen types of minerals.

Fuel for the Body

Carbohydrates provide the body with fuel. They play the same role in a human that gasoline plays in a car. All carbohydrates can be divided into two groups: simple and complex. The simplest carbohydrates are called monosaccharides. *Mono* means "one" and *saccharide* means "sugar unit." Monosaccharides are often called simple sugars. The most important simple sugar in digestion is glucose. Because glucose is found in the blood, it is sometimes called "blood sugar." The bloodstream carries glucose to every cell. Cells absorb glucose and change it to energy. Glucose is also the most widely distributed monosaccharide in food. It is found in all fruits and vegetables.

Complex carbohydrates are called polysaccharides. *Poly* means "many," and polysaccharides are made of chains containing hundreds or thousands of small sugar units. Two common complex carbohydrates found in food are starch and fiber.

Starch and Fiber

Starch and fiber in the diet come from plants. When the sun shines on plants, chlorophyll in the leaves absorbs the sun's energy. Plants also take in carbon dioxide from

Glucose, the most important monosaccharide in digestion, is found in all fruit.

Vegetables are simple carbohydrates that provide the body with fuel.

the air and water through their roots. Within the chlorophyll, plants use the energy of the sun to chemically combine carbon dioxide and water. The resulting compound is glucose. This complex chemical reaction in plants is called photosynthesis. Plants use most of their glucose for growth and development. For example, plants use some of the glucose for immediate energy and store the excess in the form of starch for future use. From glucose, plants also make fiber, a structural compound that supports stems and leaves.

Animals depend on the stored starch in plants for food energy. Starch is a complex polysaccharide that most animals, including people, can digest. Starch is essential in the diet because it is the primary source of glucose. On average, Americans eat about a half-pound of starch each day. Most grains, legumes, and roots are rich in starch. Worldwide, cereal grains such as wheat, rice, oats, millet, barley, and corn—the seeds of grasses—supply more than 50 percent of human energy. The legumes, which are seeds such as peas and beans, are also popular starchy foods in many countries. Potatoes are examples of roots that are rich in starch.

Fiber is a name given to a broad group of polysaccharides that the body cannot digest. Fiber is sometimes called roughage or bulk. Foods that contain a lot of fiber are fruits, vegetables, and the bran layers of cereal grains. Fiber is a

Seeds and cereal grains provide starch in the diet.

valuable part of the human diet, even though it is not digested. It swells in water and therefore forms a bulk against which intestinal muscles can push to retain their healthy tone. Fiber also captures several components of food such as bile acids, some food additives, and contaminants. When excreted, the fiber carries these components out of the body.

Building Materials for the Body

Whereas carbohydrates provide energy for cells, proteins provide cells with building materials for growth and maintenance. From conception, the body uses proteins to make new cells. New cells are needed for growth, and those that are damaged or lost through normal function, must be replaced using proteins.

Proteins are large molecules made from smaller units called amino acids. There are twenty-two different amino acids. Nutritionists classify amino acids into two groups: essential and nonessential. The body can make nonessential amino acids from food. However, essential amino acids cannot be created in the body and must be supplied in food. There are nine essential amino acids.

Protein in the diet comes from both plant and animal sources. Animal protein can be described as "complete" because it contains all the essential amino acids. Good sources of animal protein include milk, meat, eggs, dairy products, and seafood. Vegetable protein is usually low in one or more essential amino acids, so it is called "incomplete." However, by combining various vegetables, one can get all the essential amino acids in a meal. Some vegetables that are high in protein are nuts, legumes, and grains.

Most proteins are used to build cellular structures in the body. However, one type of protein plays a special role. Enzymes are a unique group of proteins that act as catalysts to change the rate of chemical reactions in the body. Without enzymes, chemical reactions in living things would occur too slowly to sustain life. Enzymes catalyze a variety of reactions, from digestion of foods to construction of new tissue.

Meat, eggs, and cheese are good sources of animal protein. Cashews and almonds also provide protein.

Energy Storage

Lipids, like proteins, are supplied in the diet from a variety of plant and animal sources. Lipids are a broad group of naturally occurring substances that are insoluble in water and have a greasy feel. They are commonly called fats. There are three classes of lipids: triglycerides, phospholipids, and sterols.

About 95 percent of the fatty substances in foods and in human bodies fall into the triglyceride group. Triglycerides are energy-rich nutrients that provide almost twice as much energy per serving as carbohydrates. Triglycerides are found in foods such as meat, dairy products, fish, and vegetable oils. They can be used by the body for energy or stored as fat for use in the future. Fat stored in the body plays many important roles. It surrounds and pads organs, protecting them from damage, and contains valuable fat-soluble nutrients.

The second class of fats is the phospholipid group. Phospholipids are found in the membranes that surround all cells. As their name suggests, phospholipids are lipids that contain the element phosphorus. They are important because they act as a bridge between fatty materials and water-based substances. They can serve this role because one end of a phospholipid is attracted to water while the other end is attracted to fats. Phospholipids help fats move into and out of the watery contents of cells.

Sterols are the third group of fats. Cholesterol is a critical sterol in the human body because it has so many jobs. It is a component of bile acids, which are needed in fat digestion. It is also the forerunner of sex hormones, estrogen, and testosterone. Brain and nerve cells contain cholesterol as part of their basic structure. Cholesterol is found in cell membranes and is therefore present in every cell in the body.

Vital Fluid

Macronutrients, carbohydrates, proteins, and fats would be useless without water. Even though water is not considered to be a macro- or micronutrient, it is essential for life. Water is the major component in all body fluids and makes up 55 to 60 percent of an adult's body weight. In the body, watery fluids have a variety of functions. They carry both nutrients and wastes and participate in chemical reactions. Water fills cells and the spaces between them. It dissolves chemicals, lubricates joints, and helps regulate body temperature.

In addition to the obvious dietary sources, nearly all foods contain water. The water content of food varies from 2 to 98 percent. Whether introduced into the body in food or as a beverage, water can be absorbed directly into the body without being digested or processed in any way.

A person at rest loses about forty ounces of water per day through urine, breath, and evaporation through skin. When working and sweating, a person loses even more water. Because water constantly leaves the body, it must be replaced. At the minimum, a person should drink forty ounces of water each day. If the weather is hot, more than twice that amount may be needed.

The Micronutrients and Their Supporting Roles

Vitamins play a supporting role to the macronutrients in the body. Vitamins are natural substances that are essential in tiny quantities for proper nutrition. Most vitamins act as coenzymes, which means they must be present for enzymes to do their work. Vitamins are indispensable components of hundreds of chemical reactions that convert food to energy.

A vitamin's solubility is critical. A vitamin is soluble in either water or fat. Solubility affects how the body absorbs, transports, stores, and excretes a particular vitamin. For example, water-soluble vitamins can be absorbed directly into the bloodstream and travel freely to cells. On the other hand, fat-soluble vitamins require special carrier proteins to pass through the intestinal wall to the blood. Upon reaching cells, water-soluble vitamins move easily into and out of the watery compartments of the cells. Fat-soluble vitamins tend to get trapped in fat cells. The kidneys can detect and remove surplus water-soluble vitamins. However, excess fat-soluble vitamins may remain in storage sites for long periods of time. Since they are not easily excreted, they can build up to toxic levels.

Humans must drink water every day to replenish the water they lose through urine, breath, and evaporation.

Vitamin B is one of many natural substances essential for proper nutrition.

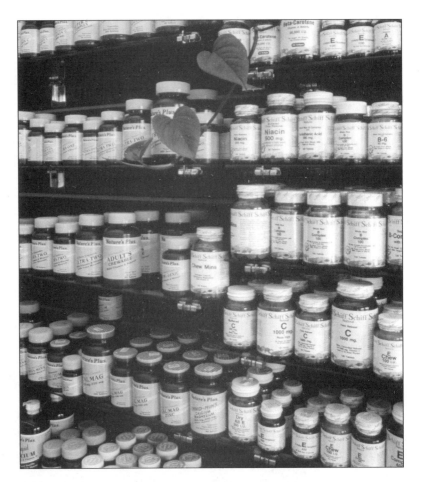

The Water-Soluble B Vitamins

One of the important water-soluble vitamins is vitamin B. Vitamin B is really a group of vitamins that includes thiamine (B_1), riboflavin (B_2), niacin (B_3), biotin, pantothenic acid (B_5), pyridoxine (B_6), folate (folic acid), and B_{12}. Most B vitamins serve as coenzymes in chemical reactions that release energy from food.

The primary function of vitamin B_1 (thiamine) is as a coenzyme for growth and reproduction. Thiamine plays a particularly important role in the normal function of nerves. Good sources of thiamine are foods such as brewer's yeast, pork, sunflower seeds, whole grains, legumes, and nuts. Lack of thiamine is rare, but it still occurs in countries where polished rice is the main food staple. Beriberi is a disease caused by a deficiency of vitamin B1. Because thiamine helps to regulate nerve processes, paralysis sets in when it is lacking in the diet. Additional symptoms of thiamine deficiency include damage to the nervous system, the heart, and other muscles.

Like thiamine, vitamin B2 (riboflavin) helps enzymes release energy from nutrients. Riboflavin is necessary for reproduction, growth, repair, development of body tissues, and immune response. Yogurt, mushrooms, ricotta and cottage cheese, spinach, and beets are great sources of riboflavin. Lack of this vitamin causes cracks and redness at the corners of the mouth, inflamed eyelids, and sensitivity to light.

Vitamin B3 (niacin) is important in the metabolism of all types of food. Niacin plays a role in maintaining the elasticity of the skin as well as promoting optimal function of the nervous and digestive systems. It is vital for the production of hormones and the repair of DNA. A few of its many sources include beef liver, tuna, mushrooms, chicken breasts, salmon, pecans, and turkey. A niacin-deficiency disease, pellagra, produces symptoms of diarrhea, vomiting, dizziness,

Symptoms of pellagra, a niacin-deficiency disease, include peeling, thickening, and discoloration of the skin.

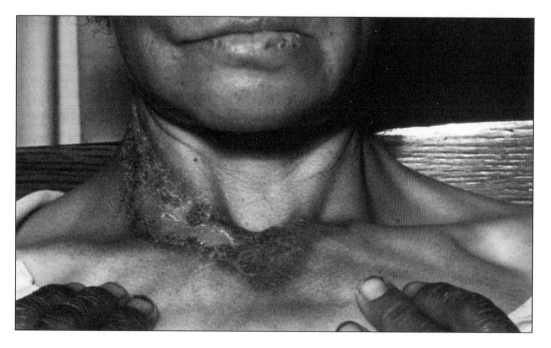

and confusion. In the early 1900s, pellagra was widespread in the southern United States. At that time, many southerners subsisted on poor, low-protein diets.

Very high doses of niacin are sometimes prescribed to treat hardening of the arteries and high cholesterol. However, such doses can be toxic and patients must be watched carefully. Large doses of niacin can produce fatigue and nausea, dilate capillaries, and cause a tingling effect that can be annoying or painful.

Biotin is not as well understood as the other B vitamins. However, scientists do know that it is essential in the replication of DNA and RNA, the materials that make up the genetic code. Biotin is found in many foods, especially egg yolks. It is made in the human digestive tract by bacteria, so biotin deficiency is rare. Symptoms of low biotin include abnormal heart action, nausea, muscle pain, and dry, scaly skin.

Vitamin B_5 (pantothenic acid) plays a role in chemical reactions that stimulate growth. Pantothenic acid is found in many foods, including meat, fish, poultry, whole grain cereals, and legumes. Though deficiencies of this vitamin are rare, a B_5 shortage can cause vomiting, diarrhea, and fatigue.

Vitamin B_6 (pyridoxine) is a coenzyme in the metabolism of fatty acids and amino acids. It also helps make niacin and is needed for the production of red blood cells. Some of the best sources of pyridoxine are green, leafy vegetables, meat, fish, poultry, fruits, legumes, and whole grains. Lack of pyridoxine can cause weakness, irritability, and insomnia. These symptoms may be seen in the elderly and in people who exercise a lot. Large doses of B_6 supplements taken for months or years can be toxic, causing irreversible nerve damage that begins with numbness in the feet and hands.

Folate (folic acid) is a coenzyme used to make DNA, so it is important in the formation of new cells. Folate is found in black-eyed peas, brewer's yeast, pinto beans, spinach, and many other common foods. People with damaged digestive systems have difficulty absorbing folate and can develop a deficiency. Two of the first symptoms of folate deficiency are anemia and further complications in the digestive tract. Folate

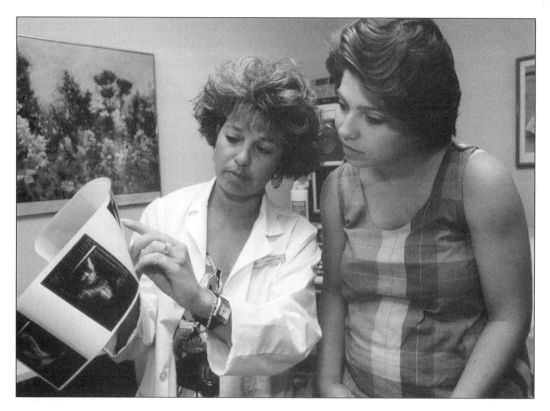

is an essential nutrient for pregnant women. Its presence in the diet prevents spina bifida, a birth defect in which the developing fetus's neural tube does not close and protect the spine.

Vitamin B$_{12}$ and folate depend on each other for activation. Vitamin B$_{12}$ is used in the production of new cells and the maintenance of nerves. Good sources of B$_{12}$ are animal products such as meats, dairy, and milk. Anemia is an early symptom of a vitamin B$_{12}$ shortage. Chronic deficiency of this vitamin can cause degeneration of nerves that leads to paralysis.

Proper medical care during pregnancy can determine a folate deficiency.

Water-Soluble Vitamin C

Another water-soluble nutrient is vitamin C. Vitamin C has a different mode of action than the B vitamins because it functions as an antioxidant. Antioxidants in cells and body fluids protect other molecules from being "oxidized" or damaged. All of the body's cells use oxygen to produce energy. During normal metabolism, some oxygen is changed to a damaging form known as a free radical. Free radicals attack and harm cells, interfering with normal cell functions. Vitamin C and other antioxidants bind with free radicals and neutralize them. Vitamin C also plays many other essential roles. It helps enzymes do their jobs, aids in absorption of iron, promotes the formation of collagen, and strengthens the body's ability to resist colds and infections.

Good food sources of vitamin C include fruits, especially citrus fruits; cabbage-type vegetables; and dark green vegetables. Lack of vitamin C in the diet can lead to scurvy, a disease that causes bleeding, loose teeth, pain, and lack of energy. If left untreated, scurvy can be fatal.

Vitamins That Accumulate in Fatty Tissue

Not all vitamins dissolve in the watery parts of cells. Vitamin A was the first fat-soluble vitamin to be recognized. Vitamin A is a versatile vitamin that plays roles in promoting vision, strong immune response, and tooth and bone growth. It also aids in the growth of healthy epithelial cells. Epithelial cells cover the entire body, inside and out. Many epithelial cells produce mucus, which lubricates body surfaces and protects against invading microorganisms. When these cells are harmed, the entire body is subject to infection.

Vitamin A is found in a variety of foods. The richest sources are liver, fish liver oils, milk and milk products, butter, and eggs. Many plants contain provitamin A, a compound that can be converted into vitamin A in the body. Vegetables and fruits are great sources of this nutrient.

Vitamin A deficiency is a major problem in developing countries where food is scarce. More than 100 million children worldwide suffer from some shortage of vitamin A, which causes them to get sick easily. An early symptom of vitamin A deficiency is night blindness. Another is thickened, dry skin that is prone to infections. Eventually, lack of vitamin A can damage all body systems.

On the other hand, too much vitamin A can cause toxicity, resulting in problems throughout the body. Toxicity rarely occurs unless someone is taking large doses of vitamin A supplements. However, since the vitamin is stored in the liver, people who eat a lot of liver may develop some toxic symptoms. Also, vitamin A acne cream, a medication that promotes new skin growth, has been known to cause birth defects when used by pregnant women.

Another fat-soluble nutrient, vitamin D, is different from all other nutrients because the body can make it with the help of sunlight. Vitamin D is also available in foods such as fortified milk, egg yolk, liver, and fatty fish. Vitamin D helps deposit minerals in bone by raising calcium and phosphorus blood levels. As with all fat-soluble vitamins, both a deficiency and an excess amount of vitamin D can cause health problems. Rickets is a disease caused by a deficiency of vitamin D that afflicts millions of children worldwide. These young people exhibit bone deformities and slow growth. Excessive amounts of vitamin D in the diet, on the other hand, may be linked to the occurrence of kidney stones.

Like vitamin C, vitamin E is an important antioxidant. While vitamin C is found in the watery parts of cells, vitamin E is found in the fatty portions. Vitamin E is found in plant oils (such as margarine and salad oils), green leafy vegetables, wheat germ, whole grain products, liver, egg yolks, nuts, and seeds. Vitamin E deficiency causes loss of function in the spinal cord and retina, resulting in poor coordination and blurred vision.

Vitamin K is best known for its role in blood clotting. It is essential in the production of four of the thirteen proteins required for clotting to occur. It also helps make bone protein as well as a protein that hinders the formation of kidney stones. Bacteria living in the large intestine manufacture a small amount of vitamin K. However, they do not supply enough, so vitamin K must be obtained from foods such as cauliflower, broccoli, cabbage, spinach, cereals, soybeans, and beef liver. Vitamin K deficiency is rare. It may be found in people who are taking large doses of antibiotics, medications that can destroy the vitamin-K-producing bacteria in their guts.

This young girl's leg bone deformities are caused by a vitamin D deficiency.

Gifts from the Earth

Like vitamins, most minerals are essential micronutrients. Minerals are unique in that they are not made by plants or animals. Minerals are inorganic elements and compounds that come from the earth. Plants absorb minerals from water and soil, and animals must eat these plants to get the minerals. When consumed by animals, minerals retain their characteristics. They cannot be changed into anything else, nor can they be destroyed by heat, air, acid, or mixing. In fact, the ash that remains when food is burned contains all the minerals that were in that food originally.

Minerals are generally placed in two categories: major minerals and trace, or minor, minerals. Major minerals are needed in the diet in larger quantities than minor minerals. Major minerals include sodium, chloride, potassium, calcium, phosphorus, magnesium, and sulfur. There are fifteen trace minerals.

Minerals That Balance Fluids

The mineral sodium helps maintain normal fluid balance in the spaces outside of cells. It also assists in the transmission of nerve impulses and in muscle contractions. Lack of sodium in the diet causes muscle cramps, fatigue, and loss of appetite. All processed foods contain a lot of sodium, especially salt and soy. Fresh fruits and vegetables contain very little. Too much sodium in the diet can cause swelling and high blood pressure.

Chloride is found in association with sodium in extracellular fluid. It too helps maintain normal fluid balance. Chloride is also found in the stomach, where it is a component of hydrochloric acid. There is plenty of chloride in foods, especially those that are processed. Therefore, deficiency of chloride is practically unknown. However, normal chloride levels may dip after periods of heavy sweating, chronic diarrhea, or vomiting.

Potassium is a mineral found inside body cells. Like sodium and chloride, potassium is important in fluid balance, and in nerve transmission. Unlike the best sources of sodium and chloride, the best sources of potassium are fruits and vegetables. Potassium deficiency is rare, but it can occur in diets low in fresh foods. It is also seen after bouts of fluid loss or dehydration. An early symptom of low potassium is muscle weakness.

Calcium and Phosphorus: The Most Abundant Minerals

There is more calcium than any other mineral in the body. Ninety-nine percent of this calcium is in the bones and teeth. Here, it plays two roles: as part of bone and tooth structure and as a calcium reserve. A calcium reserve, or bank, makes calcium readily available to the blood. For the body to function normally, calcium levels in the blood must remain constant. When calcium levels in the blood are low, the mineral is pulled from the bone calcium bank and added to the blood.

Only 1 percent of calcium, that which is not in bone, circulates in blood. Blood delivers it to cells, where it participates in several chemical reactions. Calcium helps regulate muscle contractions, clot blood, transmit nerve impulses, secrete hormones, and activate enzymes. Milk and milk products, small fish, tofu, green vegetables, and legumes are good sources of calcium. Calcium deficiency affects many body systems and can cause stunted growth in children. In adults, lack of calcium is indicated in bone loss.

Phosphorus is the second most abundant mineral in the body. About 85 percent of the body's phosphorus is found as calcium phosphate in bones and teeth. Phosphorus is also part of DNA and RNA, the molecules of genetic code that are present in most cells. Therefore, phosphorus is necessary for growth. Phosphorus also helps transfer energy during chemical reactions in cells. Many enzymes and B vitamins become active only when a phosphate group is attached. In another role, phosphorus combines with lipids to form phospholipids. These essential compounds help carry fats in the blood, and they are the major structural components of cell membranes. Animal protein is the best source of phosphorus, but it can also be obtained from egg yolks, cheese, dried peas and beans, milk products, soft drinks, and nuts. Deficiency in phosphorus can cause weakness, loss of appetite, malaise, and bone pain.

Magnesium and Sulfur: Important Parts of Protein

Like calcium and phosphorus, most magnesium is located in bone. The rest is found in muscle, soft tissues, and extracellular fluid. Magnesium is part of the protein-making machinery in cells and is also necessary for energy metabolism. Like calcium, magnesium is involved in muscle contraction and blood clotting. Magnesium is a central component of every chlorophyll molecule, so it is present in all green plants. Legumes, seeds, and nuts are primary dietary sources. Magnesium deficiency can develop in cases of alcohol abuse, protein malnutrition, kidney disease, or diseases that induce prolonged vomiting or diarrhea. It causes weakness, confusion, muscle twitches, insomnia, leg and foot cramps, and shaky hands.

Like magnesium, sulfur plays many vital roles in the body. It is present in amino acids, so it is a component of every protein and therefore found in all cells. Proteins are a large class of molecules that have a multitude of different jobs in the body. For one, proteins are the materials from which cells are made. In an entirely different role, a special group of proteins, enzymes, speed up chemical reactions. For proteins to be made in the body, sulfur must be available. Eggs are the best food source of sulfur. Sulfur is also available in meat, fish, cheese, and milk.

Just a Trace of Minerals

Unlike major minerals, trace minerals are present in the body in minute quantities. All of the trace minerals in a human would hardly fill a teaspoon. Yet each plays some vital role. A deficiency of any of these trace minerals may be fatal, and an excess of many is equally deadly.

Trace minerals include iron, zinc, iodine, selenium, copper, manganese, fluoride, chromium, molybdenum, arsenic, nickel, silicon, and boron. Of these minerals, iron may be the best known. The role of iron in good health is well known. It is a structural part of hemoglobin, the oxygen-carrying pigment in red blood cells. It is also a component in muscle protein. Excessive bleeding is one cause of low iron. Pregnancy also places heavy iron demands on women, so expectant mothers are often given iron supplements to avoid deficiency. Worldwide, lack of iron is the most common nutrient deficiency. Early symptoms include fatigue, weakness, headaches, apathy, pallor, and poor tolerance to cold.

Too much iron in the body is as dangerous as too little. Among men in the United States, iron overload is more common than iron deficiency. It is caused by a hereditary defect that allows the small intestine to absorb too much iron. As excess iron builds up in tissues, damage occurs, especially in iron-storing organs such as the liver. Iron is

Too little iodine in the diet causes the thyroid gland in the neck to enlarge, a condition known as a goiter.

also dangerous if ingested in massive amounts. Iron poisoning can result in death within four hours. Poisoning with vitamins containing iron is the second most common cause of accidental poisoning in small children (after aspirin).

Though not as well known to the general population as iron, zinc is another active trace element. It is required as a cofactor by more than one hundred enzymes. All cells contain zinc, with the highest concentrations in bone, the prostate gland, and eyes. Zinc plays important roles in the production of white blood cells, immune function, growth, and development.

The trace mineral iodine is an integral part of thyroid hormones. These hormones regulate body temperature, the rate of metabolism, growth, and nerve and muscle function. If enough iodine is not available in the diet, cells in the thyroid gland enlarge in an effort to capture every available iodine atom that travels through the body. Enlargement of the thyroid gland is called goiter. Deficiency of iodine also causes fatigue and weight gain. The best food source of iodine is seafood. Inland, iodine levels in the soil vary; some areas are very iodine-poor. To combat health problems caused by iodine deficiency, many salt distributors began adding iodine to their products in the 1930s.

Selenium is an element in an antioxidant enzyme and therefore functions much like vitamin E. The mineral is found naturally in meat and is added to many processed foods. Another mineral found in enzymes is copper. All copper-containing enzymes play roles in reactions that consume oxygen or oxygen radicals. Even though copper deficiency is rare, it has been seen in children who also have iron or protein deficiency.

Manganese, fluoride, chromium, molybdenum, arsenic, nickel, silicon, and boron are other trace minerals required by the body in minuscule amounts. The functions of these minerals are not well defined yet, but it is clear that the body cannot function without them. Deficiency of these minerals leads to health problems.

A Healthy Body

Nutritional studies have shown that a healthy diet must consist of foods that contain all food groups: carbohydrates, fats, and proteins, as well as vitamins and minerals. No single type of nutrient can sustain good health. Each is dependent on other nutrients to maintain optimal health. Cells cannot grow, repair, and divide unless they are supplied with all the materials they need.

In a well-balanced diet, every type of nutrient is available. Each nutrient group has a specific function in the body. Carbohydrates make up the bulk of the diet because they supply

Parents can teach proper nutrition by providing a well-balanced diet for their children.

cells with immediate energy. Foods rich in fats provide the body with concentrated energy and are especially important in times when food is scarce. Proteins are the molecules used to make cells and other structures in the body. Vitamins and minerals play thousands of roles as enzymes and other molecules that support chemical reactions. Careful food choices that give an appropriate balance of all nutrients are essential. Deficiency of any of the macro- or micronutrients can lead to disease.

3 Interesting Events in the Food Tube

The digestive system is always active. Sometimes the sounds and sensations that it produces can be embarrassing or confusing. Most burps, gurgles, and growls are perfectly normal. However, a few digestive events may cause alarm or discomfort.

Bad Breath

One of the most noticeable maladies of the digestive system is bad breath, or halitosis. Bad breath generally has one of two causes: oral hygiene or the food itself. Food lodged between teeth may ferment and produce bad smells. Poor oral hygiene can also cause gum disease, resulting in foul odors. Proper brushing and flossing can eliminate both of these problems. Odors from some foods, such as onions and garlic, can also cause offensive breath. The oils in these foods pass from the bloodstream into the lungs and are exhaled. This type of bad breath is temporary.

Even though most halitosis is easily eliminated, there are diseases that cause bad breath. Liver failure gives breath a mousy odor. When the kidneys stop functioning, breath smells like urine. In severe diabetes, breath smells like acetone (nail polish remover).

Choking

A more alarming condition that may occur in the upper end of the digestive tube is choking. When someone chokes,

A dentist flosses a patient's teeth. Proper flossing can prevent bad breath.

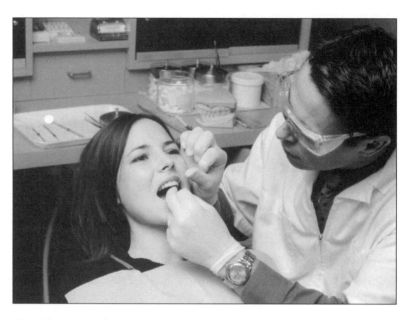

food has literally gone down the wrong way. Instead of traveling down the esophagus, it has slipped into the air passage. Usually, a cough will remove food in the airway. However, if the victim is in obvious distress and cannot make a sound, the air passage is completely blocked. This can be a life-threatening situation.

Before a rescuer tries to help a choking person, he or she must first determine if the victim can talk. If so, then the victim is getting some air. If not, quick action is needed. The victim should never be struck on the back. This may lodge the food particle even further. Instead, the rescuer should use the Heimlich maneuver. Standing behind the victim, the rescuer wraps his or her arms securely around the lower part of the victim's rib cage. The rescuer then gives a sudden, strong hug inward and upward. Hopefully, the push will expel air from the lungs and dislodge the stuck food particle. If the Heimlich doesn't work, the choking person should be positioned on his or her back. The rescuer should open the victim's mouth, lift the tongue and jaw, and use his or her fingers to remove the foreign body.

A choking person who is alone can administer the Heimlich to himself. By making a fist with one hand and placing the thumb over the diaphragm (between the lower ribs), the victim can press inward and upward with a quick motion. If this is unsuccessful, the victim should press the upper abdomen over any firm surface such as the back of a chair or a countertop.

Burping

An embarrassing, but harmless, digestive event is burping, or belching. Everyone has gas in their digestive tract. Eating or drinking allows some gas to enter the upper portion of the tract. However, eating or drinking quickly,

A man demonstrates the Heimlich maneuver.

chewing gum, or smoking lets excessive amounts of air in the stomach. Burping is the way most swallowed air leaves the stomach. Air in the stomach that is not released by a burp moves to the small intestine.

Even though occasional belches are normal, people who burp continuously may have a disorder of their upper gastrointestinal tract. If the belcher feels that releasing gas relieves the discomfort, he or she may develop a habit of belching. Sometimes, nonprescription antacids containing simethicone are used to help eliminate gas. Simethicone creates a foam that links up all the gas bubbles in the stomach so that they are more easily belched away.

Vomiting

Air is not the only thing that can be expelled from the upper GI tract. The contents of the stomach can be sent back up the esophagus. Humans have a vomiting, or emetic, center in their brains. This center gets turned on automatically when the stomach is irritated by overeating or by germs. Vomiting is the body's mechanism of ridding itself of something annoying. Spinning in circles, smelling something disgusting, or touching the back of the throat can also cause vomiting.

Once the events leading to vomiting begin, it is almost impossible to stop them. First, there is sweating, heavy salivating, and a feeling of nausea. Then the breathing tube closes to keep vomit out of the lungs. Muscles in the back of the mouth lift up and muscles at the opening of the stomach loosen. The diaphragm and chest contract strongly and squeeze the stomach. Vomit flies up the esophagus and out of the mouth. Muscle contractions may continue for several minutes to ensure that the stomach is drained. Sometimes vomiting even empties the upper part of the small intestine as well. When that happens, green bile is seen in the rejected food contents. Because vomiting causes such strong muscle contractions, the eyes may become red from pressure.

Projectile vomiting is more serious than the simple vomiting associated with nausea. In this type, stomach contents are expelled repeatedly with such force that they spray in a wide arc. Projectile vomiting usually signals a blockage or narrowing in the opening between the stomach and small intestine. Immediate medical attention is required.

Dehydration

One complication that can result from vomiting and some other digestive system problems is excessive loss of body fluids. Losing body fluids results in dehydration, a deficiency of water in the body. Dehydration occurs when the body's output of water is greater than its intake. Lack of water stimulates the brain's thirst center, causing a person to drink more water. If water intake cannot keep up with water loss, dehydration becomes more severe.

Over millions of years, the body has developed several mechanisms to save water. These natural protection techniques are controlled by feedback from the body to the brain.

The loss of water through sweating stimulates the brain's thirst center.

The body's water-saving mechanisms are designed to keep the body functioning, even under adverse conditions. To operate, the body must have some water in the brain tissue and in the blood. The body's first step in water conservation is to decrease water loss through sweating and urine. Next, the water inside of cells moves into the bloodstream. This causes tissues in the body to dry out. Eventually, cells begin to shrivel and malfunction.

When water levels in the body are extremely low, brain cells suffer. Brain cells are the most susceptible to dehydration. One sign that the brain is lacking fluids is mental confusion. If untreated, dehydration can progress to coma. For mild dehydration, drinking plain water is all that is needed. In more severe cases, intravenous fluids are required.

Pains and Growls

Most of the food, water, and gas that travels down the esophagus makes its way to the stomach and stays there. Eventually, the stomach empties of food, and the nutrients provided by that food are absorbed and used by tissues. Then, the body sends out a message that it is time to eat again. The brain interprets that message as hunger. Hunger is a more complicated feeling than just a pain in the stomach. Even people who have had their stomachs surgically removed as a result of disease still feel hungry. There is a small area in the brain, the hunger center, that senses the body's need for food.

When food is in the stomach, muscle contractions help mix it with gastric juices. When the stomach has been empty for several hours, different muscle contractions occur. These contractions are in the body of the stomach and are sometimes called "hunger pains." Hunger pains can be very strong, lasting from two to three minutes, and quite uncomfortable. They are more intense in young people because they have better GI muscle tone than older people. The muscle contractions increase when blood levels of glucose drop, usually several hours after a meal.

Hunger pains can be accompanied by growling sounds. Stomach and intestinal growling occur when there is air in the GI tract. The digestive system is a hollow tube lined with muscles that contract regularly. Between meals, muscle contractions occur along the entire length of the digestive tract. This keeps mucus and foodstuffs from accumulating at any one site. Bacteria break down food, producing gas in the process. If air bubbles and gases are trapped in the digestive tract, the contractions cause them to vibrate. These vibrations result in the growling noises associated with hunger.

Gas in the Gut

Air and gas in the digestive system that is not released by burping travels through the stomach to the small and large intestines. Here, most of it is absorbed by the body. However, some gas travels to the large intestine for release through the rectum. On average, people pass gas through the rectum fourteen times each day. This type of gas is called flatulence.

Flatulence is primarily made up of odorless vapors: carbon dioxide, oxygen, nitrogen, and hydrogen. For some reason, one-third of the population generates methane gas, which is also odorless. The unpleasant smells associated with flatulence are produced when the natural bacteria living in the large intestine break down protein. This digestive activity releases gases that smell bad because they contain sulfur.

Some foods and food residues produce more gas than others. Most of the gas-producing foods are carbohydrates, primarily sugars. For example, beans, cabbage, and brussels sprouts are a few of the foods that contain the sugar raffinose. Not everyone is able to completely digest raffinose in the small intestine, so it travels on to the large intestine, where bacteria digest it. Part of this digestive process produces gas.

There are other sugars that do not digest well in some people's bodies. Lactose, or milk sugar, is found in milk and all milk products. Many people, particularly those of African,

An eighteenth-century cartoon shows a man suffering from flatulence and indigestion. Demons encourage him to eat the foods that cause the discomfort.

Native American, or Asian background, have low levels of the enzymes needed to digest lactose. Also, as people age, they produce less of the lactose-digesting enzyme. Consequently, over time people may experience increasing amounts of gas after eating foods that contain lactose.

Fructose and sorbitol are sugars found in a variety of fruits and some vegetables. Both are used as sweeteners in beverages and dietetic foods. People deficient in the digestive enzymes for these sugars may experience gas after eating them. All starches, except for rice, produce some gas as they are digested.

Bacteria can enter the lower digestive tract through the stomach. Although most bacteria that enter through the mouth are killed when traveling through the stomach and small intestine, a few survive the journey to the large intestine. Some bacteria also enter the large intestine through the anus. Together, these bacteria form the normal population of the lower digestive tract. They live on fiber and any bits of food or food residue that are not absorbed in the small intestine.

Most foods contain some fiber. Fiber can be soluble or insoluble. Soluble fiber is found in fruits, peas, beans, and oat bran. It dissolves easily in water and takes on a gel-like texture in the intestine. Soluble fiber is not digested in the small intestine. When it reaches the large intestine, its breakdown by bacteria causes gas. Insoluble fiber, on the other hand, passes unchanged through the entire digestive system and produces very little gas. Wheat bran and some kinds of vegetables contain insoluble fiber.

Abnormally large amounts of gas may be caused by diseases that prevent carbohydrate absorption or by overactive bacteria in the colon. Medications containing activated charcoal can provide some relief. Also, the enzymes lactase and Beano can be purchased and added to food to aid in the digestion of gas-producing sugars. However, they have no effect on gas caused by the breakdown of fiber. Even though gas may be embarrassing or uncomfortable, it is rarely a health problem. The easiest way to reduce the amount of gas in the body is by modifying the diet to include fewer gas-producing foods.

End of the Line

After the digestive system has absorbed most of the food, and intestinal bacteria have consumed any leftover nutrients, there is still some material in the large intestine. This waste material is called feces or stools. It is composed of a few dissolved salts, body secretions, fiber, bacteria, and water. As stool travels through the large intestine, water is removed from it and returned to the body. By the time this waste reaches the end of its journey, it is a semisolid mass. Mucus secreted by the large intestine lubricates its movement and protects the lining of the large intestine.

Typical feces are brown, formed, soft, and about the size and shape of sausage links. Foods and vitamins can affect the appearance of stools. Normal bowel movements do not contain blood and are not black and sticky.

The amount of feces produced depends on the amount and kind of food consumed. A high-fiber diet produces a greater mass of feces than a diet made of highly refined foods. The average North American eats two to two-and-a-half gallons of food each day. Only twelve ounces of this food leaves the colon as stools.

Expelling Wastes

Artist Wim Delvoye recreated the functions of the digestive system with his room-size invention, Cloaca.

Feces in the large intestine must be removed. Like the rest of the GI tract, both the large and small intestines are muscular tubes. They contract to move food and waste through the gut toward the anus. About four times a day, muscle contractions force the stool through the colon and toward the rectum. Removal of feces from the large intestine, through the rectum, and out the anus is called defecation.

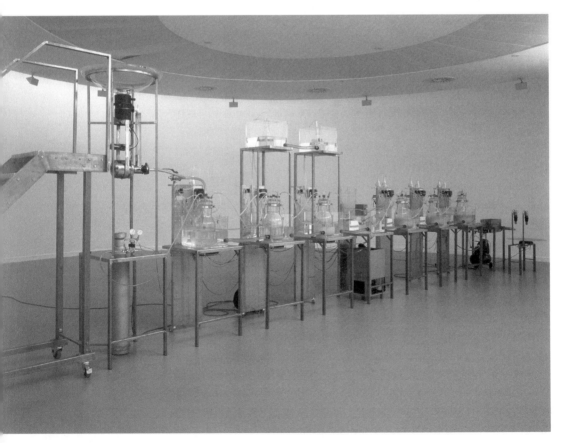

Eating triggers muscle contractions that travel throughout the gut. These contractions push stool from the colon into the rectum. This is why babies defecate after they eat. With age, people learn to control their bowels so they can decide when and where they want to pass stools.

Defecation is both a voluntary and an involuntary behavior. When stool enters the rectum, the rectum expands. Expansion stimulates a nerve that involuntarily relaxes the internal sphincter of the anus, causing the urge to defecate. The external sphincter muscles can be voluntarily tightened if necessary. When ready to move the bowels, one sits on a toilet and relaxes the external sphincters, allowing stool to pass through the anus.

Diarrhea

Usually, feces pass out of the body as semisolid masses without causing any discomfort. However, there are times when the volume of feces increases dramatically and they take on a watery consistency. This condition is called diarrhea.

Diarrhea is caused by one of two problems: Food residue moves too quickly through the intestines for water to be absorbed by the body, or water is drawn out of the walls of the intestines and is added to the food residue. In either case, the intestinal contents contain an abnormally high volume of water. Since this large volume of water is lost, the primary danger of diarrhea is dehydration.

Like vomiting, diarrhea is a normal mechanism for getting unwanted material out of the body fast. Diarrhea can have a variety of causes, including too much food or alcohol, over- or underripe raw fruits or vegetables, slightly contaminated foods, stress, or infection. Whatever the reason, in diarrhea there is faster-than-usual movement in the intestinal tract. This movement rapidly removes fecal matter from the digestive system.

Constipation

At the other extreme, there are times when fecal matter moves too slowly through the large intestine. Constipation is a condition that causes uncomfortable or infrequent bowel movements. It is accompanied by hard stools that are difficult to pass.

In constipation, feces stay in the bowel longer than normal. This allows bacteria more time to work on feces and produce large amounts of gas. During this time, the feces continue to lose water. Consequently, they form a hard mass that is difficult to evacuate.

Constipation is rarely a symptom of disease or infection. It usually occurs when one disregards the need to defecate. To relieve constipation, some people use laxatives. One group of laxatives adds bulk to stools. Examples of bulk laxatives include bran, psyllium, calcium polycarbophi, and methylcellulose. Bulk helps the intestinal muscles contract, and bulkier stools are softer and easier to pass. The use of bulking agents is one of the safest ways to promote bowel movements. They should always be accompanied by plenty of liquids.

Another group of laxatives softens stools. Stool softeners like docusate are actually detergents. They increase the amount of water that stool can hold. By decreasing the surface tension of the stool, softeners allow water to penetrate and soften feces. Mineral oil is another way to soften stool and help move it out of the body.

Osmotic agents are laxatives that pull water into the large intestine, making stool soft and loose. The extra fluid stretches the walls of the large intestine, which stimulates muscle contractions. Osmotic agents can be phosphate, magnesium, or sulfate salts, or sugars that are poorly absorbed. This type of laxative is used to clear stool before X rays or other medical tests of the digestive system.

Stimulant laxatives act directly on the walls of the large intestine and cause them to contract and move the stool. These laxatives contain irritating substances such as senna, cascara, phenolphthalein, bisacodyl, or castor oil, and may cause cramping. Prolonged use of stimulant laxatives can damage the large intestine, leading to a condition called lazy bowel.

Sometimes, constipation can be relieved by adding extra vegetables, fruits, whole grains, and water to the diet. Increasing the amount of fat in the diet can help, too. Fat boosts the secretion of bile into the duodenum. Bile's high salt content draws water from the intestinal wall, which stimulates peristalsis and softens the fecal matter. Increasing physical activity also helps stimulate bowel movements.

Malnutrition

Because of a lack of food, or because of poor food choices, some people suffer from malnutrition. In developing countries where nutritious food is not available, malnutrition is the leading cause of death in children. In countries such as the United States, malnutrition occurs when people only eat foods that have little nutritional value. It is also seen in areas of extreme poverty.

There are different magnitudes of malnutrition. One type, called marasmus, results from almost total starvation. It is usually seen in poor countries where mothers are so undernourished that they cannot produce enough milk to adequately

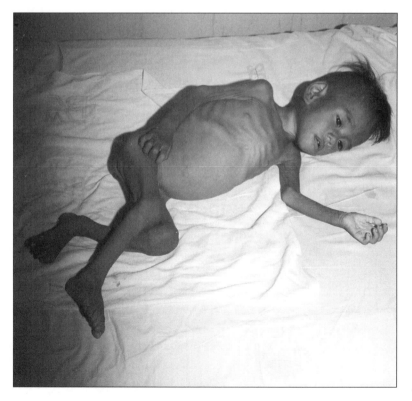

This child suffers from marasmus.

breastfeed their babies. Children suffering from marasmus are very thin from loss of muscle and body fat. Their lives are jeopardized by an injury or infection.

Another type of malnutrition, kwashiorkor, gets its name from an African word meaning "first child, second child." In a very poor family, the first child usually develops kwashiorkor when a second child is born. The first child must be weaned from breast milk needed for its sibling. In its place the older child is given food that has little nutritional value. The lack of protein in this child's diet causes the symptoms often associated with malnourished children: skin disease, discoloration of hair, retention of fluids, and slow behavioral development.

Starvation

When food is not available, starvation occurs. Starvation may result from famine, fasting, or disease. During starvation, the body continues to function as long as possible by breaking down its own tissues and using them for calories. In a short time, the internal organs and muscles are damaged, and body fat nearly disappears. During starvation, adults can lose up to half their body weight. Total starvation is fatal in eight to twelve weeks.

Obesity

A very different nutritional problem is obesity, the accumulation of excess body fat. Fat accumulates on the body when people take in more food energy than they use. The extra food energy is stored in fat cells. The prevalence of obesity in the United States has increased 33 percent in the last decade.

Scientists are not sure why some people have the tendency to become obese. Both genetic and environmental factors seem to influence body weight. In the United States, obesity is twice as common among women in lower socioeconomic groups than women in higher ones. Also, obesity is twice as common today as it was in 1900, even though the average number of calories consumed has dropped by 10 percent.

The amount of fat on a person's body reflects both the number of fat cells and the size of those cells. During the growing years, the number of fat cells multiplies. Fat cells increase more rapidly in obese children than in lean ones. By adulthood, people no longer gain new fat cells. However, fat cells can enlarge eight to ten times their original size. When fat is lost, the cells shrink in size but not in number. That is why it is difficult for people with a lot of fat cells to lose weight.

Obese people have more health challenges than lean ones. They are at a greater risk for high blood pressure, which can lead to stroke. Obesity has also been linked to heart disease and diabetes. Some forms of cancer, such as cancer of the colon, prostate cancer in men, and uterine and breast cancers in women, are more common in obese individuals.

The Sounds and Sensations of Digestion

The digestive system is very efficient at digesting food and preparing it for body cells. Sometimes it can be heard churning its contents and moving them along the GI tract. It may also be noticed when it eliminates gases. Digestive processes take in air with food and generate gases as that food is digested. These gases must leave the body, and they do so through the mouth as belches and through the anus as flatulence. Although such events can be embarrassing, they are rarely causes for concern.

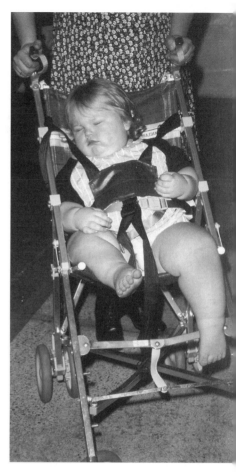

Fat cells increase more rapidly in obese children than in lean ones.

Of a more serious nature are gastric disturbances such as diarrhea and vomiting that cause loss of body fluids. These incidents may indicate that something in the body is not working correctly, and so they warrant attention. An understanding of conditions that are a normal part of day-to-day digestion, and those that are not, can help people make wise decisions about their own health. Many times mild digestive disorders can lead to, or indicate, more serious problems.

Difficulties in the Digestive System

4

A variety of diseases and disorders occur in the digestive system. This complex system of organs is vulnerable to problems at every level. From the mouth to the anus, each part of the digestive system plays a critical role in nutrient breakdown and absorption. A dysfunction at any level disrupts the entire system. Some of the disorders of the digestive system are preventable through good nutrition and hygiene. Others are more difficult to avoid because they are linked to genetics, infectious agents, or the environment.

Maladies of the Mouth

The digestive system begins with the mouth. This cavity houses teeth, gums, and other digestive structures. Gingival tissues, or gums, are common sites of infection. Both the teeth and gums are susceptible to dental plaque. Plaque is a film, or layer of material, composed of sugar, bacteria, and other debris that can adhere to the teeth and gums. As dental plaque builds up, it hardens into a solid called calculus or tartar. Tartar interferes with the seal between the gums and teeth. This puts the gums at risk of infection.

The first signs of gum infection, or gingivitis, are redness, swelling, and bleeding. Removal of the tartar can reverse gingivitis. However, if the tartar remains, this disorder gets progressively worse. Eventually, bacteria invade the bone around the teeth and cause pockets of infection. Over time, the bone slowly dissolves and the condition becomes known as periodontal disease.

Dentists estimate that periodontal disease accounts for 80 to 90 percent of all tooth loss in adults. However, when diagnosed and treated early, teeth can usually be saved. Special dentists called periodontists scale and clean the teeth and prescribe antibiotics for infection of the gums. This treatment helps the gums reattach to the teeth. After therapy, patients learn to remove tartar from their teeth by frequent brushing, flossing, and rinsing with salt or hydrogen peroxide solutions. Good dental hygiene can prevent periodontal disease. Dentists teach everyone to brush and floss regularly to prevent gingivitis and periodontal disease.

Esophageal Burn

Disorders can also develop in the esophagus, the tube connecting the mouth and stomach. In some people, gastric juice from the stomach spews into the esophagus. This produces a radiating pain that feels like it is coming from below the sternum, or breastbone. This pain is often called heartburn. Heartburn is rarely life threatening, but it can be extremely uncomfortable. In severe cases, people cannot distinguish the pain of heartburn from the symptoms of a heart attack. Most people suffer from mild heartburn at some time during their lives. Heartburn can result from overeating or drinking alcohol. Running after a meal may also force acidic stomach contents upward into the esophagus.

A condition called gastroesophageal reflux disease (GERD) also causes heartburn. In GERD, the sphincter at the lower end of the esophagus malfunctions by failing to close completely after food passes through it. As a result, hydrochloric acid from the stomach flows into the lower esophagus. Doctors recommend that people with GERD avoid foods that stimulate secretion of stomach acid such as coffee, chocolate, tomatoes, fatty foods, onions, and peppermint candy.

Heartburn is also common in people with hiatal hernias. This type of hernia is a structural abnormality in which the upper part of the stomach protrudes above the diaphragm. This condition allows gastric juices to flow upward into the esophagus. If a person with a hiatal hernia lies down after eating, it makes the heartburn much worse. Over a long period of time, the regular contact of gastric juices with the lining of the esophagus can result in inflammation and esophageal ulcers.

Bellyaches

As heartburn sufferers know, the chemicals in the stomach are very caustic. The inside of the stomach itself is a harsh environment. It contains acidic gastric juices and protein-digesting enzymes. The walls of the stomach are protected from these chemicals by thick mucus. This mucus prevents the stomach from literally consuming itself.

Sometimes, the mucous coating of the stomach lining is penetrated by acidic stomach contents. When this happens, the underlying tissues become inflamed, leading to a condition called gastritis. Continuous damage to these tissues can result in erosion of the stomach wall. These eroded areas are known as ulcers. Ulcers cause a gnawing pain that is usually felt a few hours after a meal. Eating again can relieve the pain. Ulcers are rarely life threatening, but they are dangerous if they bleed excessively.

Several factors contribute to the development of gastric ulcers. Oversecretion of gastric juices or undersecretion of protective mucus can lead to ulcer formation. Aspirin, ibuprofen, alcohol, and coffee can also interfere with the proper release of gastric juice and mucus in the stomach. Stress and smoking have been linked to this problem as well.

Recent studies have implicated a bacterium as the cause of recurring gastric ulcers. This corkscrew-shaped organism, *Helicobacter pylori,* is resistant to acid. It can attach to and destroy cells on the inside surface of the stomach. Research indicates that these bacteria do their damage by releasing enzymes and toxins that destroy the cells lining the stomach's inner wall.

In the past, patients were often instructed to consume milk products to soothe the pain of ulcers. Scientists now realize that dairy products are not good for ulcers. These products neutralize the acidity of the stomach for a short time. But in response, the stomach attempts to return to an acidic condition, so it produces more acid. Today, people with gastric ulcers take medications that inhibit the secretion of hydrochloric acid. People who have stomach ulcers caused by bacteria take antibiotics, acid inhibitors, and bismuth. This combination kills the embedded bacteria, promotes healing of the sores, and prevents recurrence.

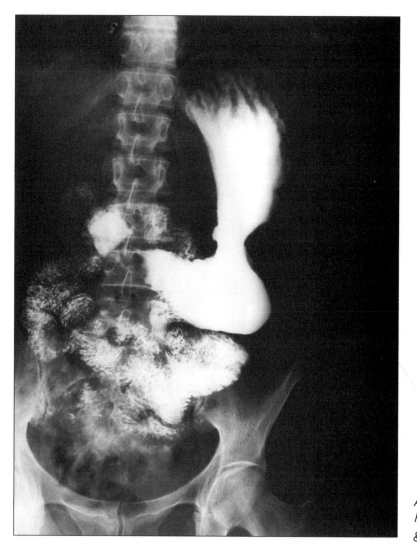

Abdominal X rays help doctors diagnose gastric ulcers.

Problems in the Liver

On its journey through the digestive system, food never enters the liver. However, without the liver, digestion could not take place. That is why a strong, vigorous liver is a vital component of a healthy digestive system. Yet the liver can suffer from disease, too. An inflammatory disease of the liver is hepatitis. It can be caused by several factors, such as viruses, medications, or chemicals.

One viral form of this disease, hepatitis A, usually occurs in children and young adults. This type of hepatitis is spread through fecal contamination of food, eating utensils, toys, or water. A person gets hepatitis A by placing a contaminated object in his or her mouth. Because hepatitis A is spread easily, restaurants require all employees to wash their hands before handling food.

Symptoms of hepatitis A include weakness, nausea, abdominal pain, and jaundice (yellowing of the skin). The disease is easily diagnosed with a blood test. Most people recover from this disease within four to six weeks with no lasting liver damage. There is a vaccine for hepatitis A that is recommended for those who work in high-risk areas such as doctors' offices, hospitals, and day-care centers.

Even though its symptoms are very similar to those of hepatitis A, hepatitis B is a more serious form of this disease. It is also caused by a virus, and accounts for about 40 percent of all hepatitis cases in the United States. Hepatitis B is spread through viral contamination of saliva, blood, or semen. It can be transmitted through blood transfusions, sexual activities, and by sharing personal items such as toothbrushes or hypodermic needles. Tattooing or body piercing with unsterilized needles is another way to catch the virus.

Although recovery time is longer for hepatitis B than for hepatitis A, the majority of people with this infection recuperate. Sometimes a blood test is all that is needed to diagnose hepatitis B. In other cases, a liver biopsy is required. In a biopsy, a small piece of the liver is removed with a needle, and the sample is examined to determine if the virus is present. Even after they recover, people who have been infected

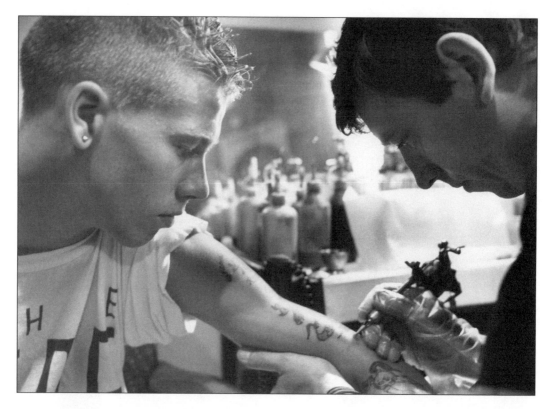

with hepatitis B retain the virus in their bodies. Because they can still transmit the virus to others, these people are referred to as carriers.

Hepatitis B can be contracted from unsterilized needles during tattooing.

Many scientists speculate that people who carry the hepatitis B virus are more prone to the fatal liver disease cirrhosis. Drugs such as interferon can be given to help fight hepatitis B infections, and vaccines against hepatitis B are now available. Individuals can protect themselves by practicing safe sex and by avoiding situations where needles used for drugs, tattoos, and body piercing may not be sanitary.

The symptoms and manifestations of hepatitis C are very much like those of hepatitis B. Like hepatitis B, this liver disease is spread by drug users who share needles. However, it is rarely transmitted by sexual contact. Most of the people who acquire hepatitis from blood transfusions are infected with the hepatitis C virus. The hepatitis C virus has an incubation period that can be as short as two weeks or as long as six months. Infection can lead to other chronic liver diseases such as cirrhosis and liver cancer.

Gallstones are another liver-related medical problem. The liver manufactures bile and stores it in the gallbladder. As fatty food travels through the small intestine, the gallbladder releases bile to aid in fat digestion. While bile is stored in the gallbladder, it becomes concentrated because the body removes excess water from it.

Bile contains a lot of cholesterol, which normally remains in a liquid form. If bile salt levels are low or if too much cholesterol is present, the cholesterol may become insoluble and form crystals. These cholesterol crystals are commonly known as gallstones. If the crystals lodge in the duct leading from the gallbladder to the small intestine, severe pain can result. The pain is usually located in the upper right area of the abdomen, and is sometimes felt in the right shoulder blade. Even though they are painful, gallstones are rarely life threatening. They can usually be removed or treated.

These human gallstones are each 3/4 inches in diameter.

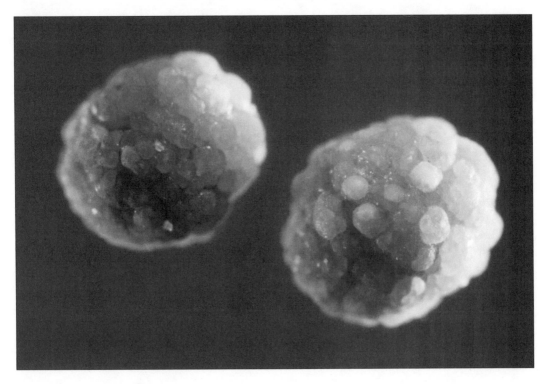

Cirrhosis of the Liver

Gallstones and hepatitis are two of the many factors that can cause cirrhosis of the liver. Others include alcoholism, drugs, infections, and buildup of fat in the liver from diabetes, malnutrition, obesity, or heart disease. In cirrhosis, scar tissue replaces normal, healthy liver tissue. Scar tissue blocks the flow of blood through the liver and prevents the organ from carrying out its normal functions.

In the United States, alcoholism is a common cause of cirrhosis. Alcoholic cirrhosis usually occurs after ten years or more of heavy drinking. The definition of "heavy drinking" varies greatly from one person to the next. In women, as few as two or three drinks a day can lead to cirrhosis. Alcohol damages the liver by interfering with the normal metabolism of proteins, fats, and carbohydrates.

Symptoms of cirrhosis vary, depending on which part of the liver is damaged. As normal tissue is lost, liver function decreases. Symptoms usually worsen over time. Initially, a person may experience fatigue, weakness, loss of appetite, nausea, and weight loss. Later, water may accumulate in the abdominal cavity and legs, causing swelling. As the liver loses its ability to make proteins essential for blood clotting, a person may bruise or bleed easily. Jaundice occurs when the liver can no longer process bile pigments. Bile deposited under the skin causes intense itching. If bile cannot reach the gallbladder, gallstones may form in bile ducts.

A severely damaged liver can no longer remove toxins from the blood. The toxins accumulate in the bloodstream and brain, causing personality changes such as forgetfulness and the inability to concentrate. As toxin levels increase, coma and death can result. Cirrhosis also slows the liver's normal ability to remove medications from the blood. Consequently, drugs build up in the blood and continue to act on the body. This causes a person with cirrhosis to be very sensitive to the medications or their side effects.

Once liver tissue is damaged, it cannot be repaired. Therefore, treatment of cirrhosis focuses on stopping the disease and delaying further harm. The type of treatment needed depends on the cause of cirrhosis. In all cases, it is essential for the patient to follow a healthy diet and to avoid alcohol. The body needs a good supply of nutrients to recover and remain healthy; alcohol only leads to continued liver damage. If the liver is so damaged that it cannot function at all, a liver transplant is necessary. In a transplant, a diseased liver is removed and replaced with a healthy one.

Pancreatitis

The pancreas, like the liver, is an accessory digestive organ. Food does not travel through it. The pancreas provides many of the digestive enzymes used in the small intestine. Any disease that disrupts the function of the pancreas severely interferes with the digestion of food. Normally, the pancreas sends pancreatic juice through a duct to the small intestine. The digestive enzymes in this juice are inactive while in the pancreas and pancreatic duct. They become activated once they reach the small intestine.

Pancreatitis is a serious condition in which the pancreas is swollen. When the pancreas is so swollen that it cannot release its digestive enzymes, the enzymes become trapped within the pancreas. Scientists do not know why, but these trapped enzymes become activated and begin to eat away at the pancreas itself. As a result, some parts of the pancreas are destroyed while other parts are badly damaged. In severe cases, digestive enzymes leak out of the damaged pancreas into the abdominal cavity. They can injure blood vessels and organs in the immediate area.

There are several factors that can trigger pancreatitis. More than 80 percent of cases are caused by either excessive use of alcohol or gallstone disease. When gallstones form, they can block the pancreatic duct and shut off the normal flow of digestive enzymes. Alcohol consumed over a long period of time can cause the pancreatic duct to clog.

Symptoms of pancreatitis often begin with a sharp abdominal pain that can linger for days. Nausea and vomiting usually occur. Without the pancreatic juices in the digestive system, digestion of fats is severely impaired. Fatty food in the intestine remains undigested. It travels to the large intestine and becomes part of the feces. Bowel movements may produce greasy stool with a foul odor.

Appendicitis

Food finishes its journey through the digestive system in the small and large intestines. Because these organs are physically long, they are prone to many problems. The proper function of the intestines is essential for digestion. The small and large intestines can develop disorders that vary from simply uncomfortable to life threatening.

In the large intestine near its junction with the small intestine, there is a small, worm-shaped organ called the appendix. The appendix does not have a digestive function, but it does contain lymph tissue that plays a role in the body's immune system. As food travels through the intestine, material can become accidentally lodged in the appendix. Bacteria can also accumulate there. When this happens, the appendix becomes inflamed and painful, a condition called appendicitis.

Symptoms of appendicitis vary greatly from person to person. Pain in the abdomen is the first sign in many individuals. Eventually, the pain localizes to the lower right part of the abdomen. Other symptoms are loss of appetite, nausea, vomiting, and fever. Adolescents are most likely to suffer from appendicitis because the opening to the appendix is large during the teen years. An inflamed appendix needs to be surgically removed by a procedure called an appendectomy. If surgery is not performed quickly, the appendix can rupture in as little as thirty-six hours. Rupture can lead to serious health problems because it releases bacteria into the abdomen.

Crohn's Disease

The appendix is not the only area of the intestine that can become inflamed and tender. The intestinal wall is subject to many different types of inflammation. People who have Crohn's disease suffer from inflammation in the lower end of the small intestine or in the large intestine. In this disorder, the intestinal wall becomes thick, reducing the diameter of the intestine. Intestinal blockages, abscesses, and painful masses may appear. Usually, the disease begins before age thirty.

Symptoms of Crohn's disease vary, but there are some common traits such as chronic diarrhea, pain in the abdomen, weight loss, and fever. Diarrhea may alternate with episodes of constipation. After a period of illness, symptoms may disappear for a long time. They usually reappear at irregular intervals through a person's life.

There is no cure for Crohn's disease, but medications can reduce swelling and pain. During episodes of constipation, stool softeners are given. Antibiotics may be needed to kill a wide variety of bacteria that can grow in the intestine. Drugs that reduce inflammation make the patient feel better and improve the appetite. People with Crohn's disease usually have a normal life span but are more likely than the general population to develop cancer of the digestive tract.

Inflamed Intestinal Pouches

Any part of the wall of the large intestine can develop a weak place that bulges into a saclike pouch. When one or more of these pouches develop, a person is said to have diverticulosis. The sigmoid part of the colon, just above the rectum, is the most common site of diverticulosis. The pouches can vary greatly in size, from as small as one-tenth of an inch to as large as six inches in diameter. If feces and bacteria get pushed into the pouches, they can become infected and inflamed. This condition is then referred to as diverticulitis.

A mild case of diverticulitis can be treated with rest, plenty of liquids, and antibiotics. Once the patient is feeling better, he or she is often put on a high-fiber diet. Severe diverticulitis causes pain, tenderness in the abdomen, and fever. In extreme cases, inflamed pouches can extend from the intestine to other organs such as the bladder. An abnormal connection can grow between the pouches and the organs they touch. This connection allows feces to move into other organs, causing infection. Another serious complication of diverticulitis is infection that results from a pouch that bursts and releases its fecal matter into the body. Intravenous antibiotics and surgery may be required.

Reason for Concern

Discomfort in any part of the digestive system may indicate a problem. Awareness of diseases helps people recognize their symptoms and know when to seek medical help. Some digestive disorders can be prevented by good hygiene and nutrition. Others occur for no apparent reason.

Digestive disorders are found from the mouth to the anus. Periodontal disease of gums causes pain and loss of teeth. Misplaced stomach acid in the esophagus produces heartburn. The same acid can create ulcers in the stomach itself. Liver and pancreatic diseases can impair function of the accessory digestive organs and interfere with normal life. Intestinal disorders can vary in severity from annoying to life threatening. Any problem that causes dysfunction of the digestive system is reason for concern and attention.

The Technological Window into the Digestive System

5

Most of the human digestive system is concealed within the body. So, external examinations by doctors are often not enough to determine the cause of digestive disorders. When a patient with a gastrointestinal complaint sees a physician, an investigation begins. The physician pieces together bits of information to find the root of the problem. First, the patient describes any troubling symptoms. Then a medical history is taken to determine whether digestive diseases run in the patient's family. Finally, the doctor does an external physical exam. This may involve listening to the stomach and intestines with a stethoscope to see if they are producing normal gut sounds and feeling the abdomen in search of swollen or tender masses.

If these preliminary questions and external exams do not give the physician enough information, medical tests may be in order. These procedures help reveal and treat problems within the GI tract. Years ago, the only way a physician could examine the digestive organs was through surgery. Today, there are many ways to explore, diagnose, and treat disorders within the digestive system. These processes can be grouped into four categories: intubation, endoscopy, imaging, and chemical measurements. Each technique provides unique clues about the health of the digestive system.

Tubes That Take Samples and Deliver Medicine

One relatively simple way to get information about the digestive system is through intubation. In this process, a thin plastic tube is passed through the nose or mouth into the stomach and small intestine. There are many uses for this procedure. From a tube in the stomach, a physician can obtain some of its contents. These can be tested for the presence of blood, analyzed for excess acidity, or evaluated for foreign materials. In the case of poisoning, a tube in the stomach can provide a sample of the poison for identification.

A doctor listens to the gut sounds of his patient through a stethoscope.

Intubation is also used in some medical treatments. For example, cool water supplied through the tube can help stop bleeding in the stomach. Liquid food can be delivered to the stomach for patients that cannot eat. If the patient's stomach is filled with dangerous material, it can be removed through the tube. In poisoning, it is a common treatment to pump out the contents of the victim's stomach. To do so, the tube is attached to a suction device that quickly removes the toxic material.

A View Within

Another type of tube that gives access to internal organs is an endoscope. An endoscope is a long flexible cylinder that contains fiber-optic light cables. An endoscope has a diameter of a quarter-inch to a half-inch, and varies from one to five feet long. It can be inserted through a body opening and steered to its destination by turning wheels on a handset. These wheels operate wires that extend through the entire endoscope. An endoscope passed into

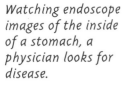

Watching endoscope images of the inside of a stomach, a physician looks for disease.

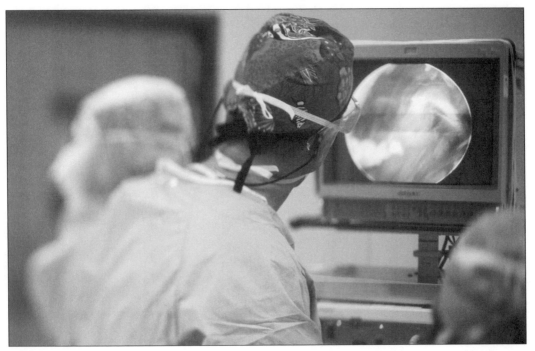

the esophagus, stomach, and small intestine can search for problems such as abnormal growths, ulcers, or inflamed tissue.

Before an endoscopy, a patient fasts for six to twelve hours so that the digestive tract is empty. Just before the tube is inserted, an anesthetic is sprayed in the throat to stop the gag reflex. Then a doctor gently guides the endoscope into the mouth and down the esophagus. By direct observation, a physician can often distinguish normal from abnormal tissue. A physician looks for any abnormal variations that might indicate disease. A healthy esophagus has a yellow-pink lining and many visible blood vessels. Once the esophagus has been examined, the endoscope can be pushed into the stomach. In an empty stomach, muscular folds of the stomach wall can be seen. The tube can then be passed into the duodenum or small intestine. This area normally has a velvety appearance due to villi on the intestinal walls.

In a procedure called a colonoscopy, an endoscope is used to examine the large intestine. Before this process, the patient takes a laxative to clean out the intestinal tract. Then the flexible tube is passed through the anus and rectum into the large intestine. Normally, the large intestine appears pink or orange. Physicians look for any variations in this color, as well as abnormal growths or bleeding. A colonoscopy can help diagnose conditions such as Crohn's disease, cancer, and diverticulitis.

The endoscope is not limited to just examining areas inside the body. It can also be used for treatment. For example, a doctor can insert a tweezerlike device through the tube to snip samples of tissue. Special brushes can also be lowered through the scope to collect cells. These cells and tissues are sent to a lab to be examined.

Camera in a Pill

In the near future, a new option will be available for examining the digestive tract. Scientists have found a way to place a camera, light source, radio transmitter, and batteries in a tiny sealed container that is about an inch long and less than half an inch wide. This container looks like a pill and is small enough to be swallowed. As it travels through the digestive system, it sends signals back to a receiver. These signals are translated to images that can be downloaded to a computer for viewing.

The camera–pill device has been through extensive animal testing and is beginning its trials in humans. There are several advantages to using this procedure in humans. For one thing, it is a much more comfortable method of viewing the digestive tract than endoscopy. Patients continue their normal daily routine as the pill travels through them. The batteries in the camera last for about six hours, the time it takes for material to move from the stomach to the upper end of the intestines. The camera pill is disposable, so after being eliminated in the stools, it does not have to be recovered.

A Camera in Surgery

Endoscopes are not only introduced into the body through natural body openings. They can also be inserted through small incisions in a procedure called laparoscopy. This technique is used to view the inside of the abdominal cavity or to perform surgery in that area. During laparoscopy, a patient is given general anesthesia.

The initial incision is usually made near the navel. Then, a tube containing a tiny camera is pushed in the opening. Images from the tip of the scope are transmitted by electrical cable to cameras or video cameras for easy viewing by the medical team. An inert gas is pumped into the body cavity to lift the abdominal wall away from the internal organs. This gives a better view of the internal structures. The gas is removed when the laparoscopic work is complete. If surgery is to be performed, other incisions are made in the abdomen for surgical instruments.

Gallstones can be removed by a laparoscopic technique. Gallstones are a common and painful problem for thousands of people. In the past, surgical removal of the gallbladder was the only treatment. This required a relatively large cut in the abdomen, followed by a long period of rest and healing.

Since its introduction, laparoscopic surgery has radically changed this practice. Ninety percent of all gallbladders are removed by this technique. First, small incisions are made in the abdomen. The endoscope is placed through one incision so the surgeon can see. A scalpel threaded through a tube is inserted in another incision. After this equipment is in place, the gallbladder is snipped away and removed.

The Laser Scalpel

Lasers can also be threaded through an endoscope and used in laparoscopic surgery. Laser surgery has many advantages over traditional surgery. It is usually faster and

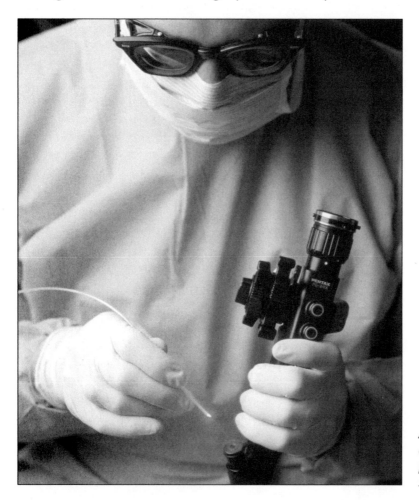

A surgeon assembles a laser endoscope in preparation for surgery.

safer, and the patient has a shorter recovery time. Laser surgery is sometimes referred to as "bloodless" surgery because tumors or other abnormalities can be removed without the use of a scalpel or scissors.

The word *laser* stands for "light, amplification by stimulated, emission of radiation." Inside a laser, an energy source excites the atoms in a special laser material. Once excited, these atoms give off light. Laser light is different from regular, white light. Ordinary light waves are irregular, and they spread out in many directions. Laser light waves are all identical and can be focused as powerful beams into a small area.

When laser light hits living tissue, it heats the water in that tissue. This converts the laser's light energy to heat energy. At high energy levels, laser light vaporizes tissue, cutting it. This is the type of energy used in a "laser scalpel." Tumors in the esophagus or other areas can be cut away with this technique. At low energy levels, laser light kills only a few cells and coagulates the blood around them. In this way, it can weld together nerves or blood vessels.

Pictures from Within

Direct views of digestive organs are not always essential. Sometimes physicians can learn a lot about an organ's condition by observing it through X rays. X-ray pictures reveal body structures in various shades of gray: Bone is white, soft tissue is light gray, fat is dark gray, and air appears black. There are several X-ray techniques for producing images of the digestive tract and accessory digestive organs. Standard abdominal X rays can show obstructions in the digestive system, such as gallstones. They can also reveal enlargement of the liver and pancreas.

Barium studies often provide more information. Barium is a material that produces a strong contrast on X-ray film; it appears as white. To enable the visualization of certain areas of the digestive system, the patient is given barium before the X rays are taken. For example, in a barium swallow or esophagography, the patient drinks a thin mixture that contains barium sulfate. On the X ray, the barium sulfate outlines the

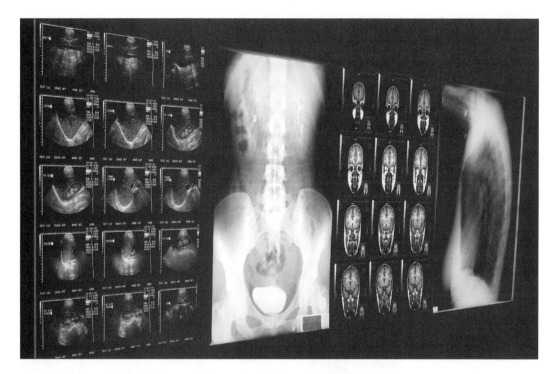

upper GI tract and helps reveal its size, shape, and condition. The barium collects in abnormal areas, highlighting conditions such as ulcers and tumors. After the patient drinks the mixture, he or she is placed on a tilting table so that films can be made from various positions.

Various types of X rays enable a doctor to see and diagnose diseases of the digestive system.

The same part of the upper GI tract can be examined using a different X-ray technique called fluoroscopy. In this procedure, as barium sulfate passes through the esophagus, stomach, and small intestine, the X rays are projected onto a fluoroscope. A fluoroscope is a specialized screen that permits continuous observation of material in motion. By observing the barium traveling through the digestive system, physicians can see how the esophagus and stomach function. This method shows whether or not food is getting blocked on its journey through the system. It also helps detect obstructions in the upper end of the digestive system.

Barium sulfate and X rays are also used to examine the lower end of the digestive system in a test called a lower gastrointestinal series, or a barium enema. Before this test, the patient is given laxatives to clean the bowels of all feces. During the test, the patient receives an enema containing barium. The barium is observed with X rays or fluoroscopy. X-ray pictures can reveal tumors, blockages, or other abnormalities. Next, the patient is taken to a toilet to expel as much of the barium as possible. Then additional X rays are made to assess colonic emptying. Barium given by mouth or enema usually causes constipation. To help eliminate it from the system, patients are given a laxative.

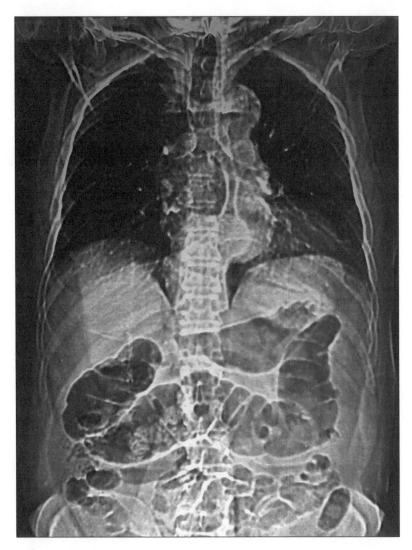

The stomach and colon appear free of disease in this CT scan of a patient's thorax and abdomen.

Most organs and ducts of the digestive system can be observed in similar X-ray tests. In each test, barium or some other contrast media is injected into the area to be studied. The gallbladder, pancreas, liver, and ducts can all be visualized with X rays and fluoroscopy. For example, to study how well the gallbladder empties bile into the duodenum, contrast medium is injected into the gallbladder. Then a fat stimulus is administered. This causes the gallbladder to contract and empty the contrast medium and bile into the bile duct and small intestine.

Sophisticated, three-dimensional X rays of the body are made with a computerized axial tomography (CT) scan. CT scans of the abdomen and pelvis create images of the liver, pancreas, and gallbladder. During a CT scan, multiple X rays pass through the area being examined. They are recorded in a computer that reconstructs the data as a two-dimensional image on a TV screen. Contrast media like barium can be injected into areas of interest to give clearer images. CT scans are important in detecting conditions such as a fatty liver and abnormally dense liver tissue.

Another, less expensive way of producing images of internal organs is with ultrasound scanning. Ultrasound equipment sends high-frequency sound waves into the area to be studied. A technician moves a small probe over the patient's abdomen, directing sound waves to various parts of the abdominal cavity. The sound waves strike organs and produce echoes. These echoes are detected and changed to electrical impulses. Then they are amplified with a transducer that displays them as images on a screen. The images can help physicians determine whether the size, shape, and positions of the accessory digestive organs are normal. Such information provides clues about undiagnosed digestive disorders. The procedure can also reveal gallstones, an enlarged gallbladder, polyps, and cancerous tissue.

In many cases, ultrasound scanning has replaced the need for CT scans. It reveals much of the same information, is less expensive, and is painless. Because ultrasound scans do not use X rays, as CT scans do, they are also safer.

One innovative use of ultrasound waves is called lithotripsy, a nonsurgical technique for getting rid of gallstones. A lithotripsy machine focuses sound waves on the gallstones. The energy of the sound waves breaks the stones into sand-sized pieces that can pass out of the gallbladder or ducts into the small intestine.

Radiation Images

Radioactive imaging is another way to study the internal digestive organs. Radioactive materials emit energy that can be detected. Preparations of radioactive solutions can be injected into organs of the digestive system. Radiation detectors can then reveal the movement of this injected material as it travels through the body. This method can be used to diagnose a diseased liver. For example, cirrhosis and hepatitis cause distinctive changes in the liver that can be seen by radioactive imaging. Cysts, abscesses, and tumors do not take up the radioactive solutions and appear on the image as defects.

Pictures from Magnets

Another way to view internal organs is through magnetic resonance imaging (MRI). Like CT scans MRIs produce pictures of internal organs. During an MRI, a patient lies on a table that is surrounded by coils of giant electromagnets. This magnetizes the patient's body, causing all of the hydrogen atoms to line up in one direction. These hydrogen atoms are in abundance wherever fat or water is present. Radio waves are then fired into the tissue being examined. Different body tissues respond by giving off radio waves of varying frequencies. A powerful computer collects and analyzes these re-emitted radio frequencies. The final information is displayed as a color picture on the computer screen. Areas of high hydrogen-atom density can be clearly distinguished from less dense regions.

Some drawbacks of MRIs are that they are more expensive than CT scans and they take longer. Occasionally, MRIs make people nervous. Some patients find that the chamber they must lie in during an MRI is confining and a little scary. The newest MRI machines have open chambers to avoid this problem.

Despite these downsides, MRIs offer many advantages and are essential tools for diagnosing some diseases. In MRI procedures, the patient is not exposed to radiation and does not need contrast media added to the body. MRIs produce far clearer images than X rays or radioactive imaging tests. Using MRI images, doctors are often able to visualize minute tumors of the digestive tract that are missed by conventional X rays or even CT scans. MRIs are essential in detecting hard-to-diagnose abnormalities of the liver.

Answers from Chemistry

Bleeding in the digestive tract can be caused by several factors. It may be due to a simple problem such as mucous membrane irritation. However, bleeding might indicate the presence of disease. If bleeding is slight, patients are often

While a patient moves through an MRI machine (upper left) a technician watches and adjusts the process on a computer monitor.

unaware of it. When it is heavy, one might vomit blood or find bright red blood in their stools.

Very small amounts of blood in stools can be detected chemically and can give clues to the presence of digestive system disorders. During a rectal exam, a physician can remove a small sample of stool with a gloved finger. This sample is placed on a piece of cardboard that has been soaked in chemicals. If blood is present in the sample, the chemicals cause it to change color. A stool sample can also be taken at home. The patient places very small amounts of stool from three different bowel movements on three different filter papers. These are mailed back to the doctor in special containers. The samples are sent to a lab. If blood is found, more testing may be required.

A Well-Ordered System

Food is a complex mixture that would be useless if it were not broken down into small units. The digestive system makes the individual components of food available to cells. It changes carbohydrates into simple sugars, proteins into amino acids, and lipids into fatty acids and glycerides. These components of food travel from the digestive system to the blood. The blood carries them to the cells of the body. There, they are converted into cell structures and life-sustaining energy.

For the building blocks of food to reach cells, all parts of the digestive system must work together. Unfortunately, disease and disorder can interrupt the normal flow of food through the body. Some digestive problems are mild, but others are life threatening. Medical technology makes it possible to diagnose disorders and administer treatments that were not available just a few years ago. Consequently, people are living longer, healthier lives than ever before.

GLOSSARY

alkaline: Basic; not neutral or acidic.

amino acids: Nitrogen-containing organic molecules that are the building blocks of proteins.

anesthetic: Medication that causes a loss of sensation.

cirrhosis: A disease of the liver that results in liver failure.

diaphragm: The layer of muscle that separates the chest cavity from the abdominal cavity.

duct: A canal or passage.

enema: An injection of liquid into the rectum.

enzyme: A protein that acts as a catalyst in biochemical reactions.

extracellular: The space outside of the cell membrane.

hard palate: The section of the roof of the mouth made of bone.

interferon: A protein that protects the body from viral invasion.

involuntary: Acting without choice; not willed.

legume: A bean, pea, or related plant.

mucous membrane: The membrane lining the digestive system that secretes mucus.

mucus: Thick, sticky liquid made by specialized cells as a lubricant or protective coating.

nasal cavity: The hollow space over the roof of the mouth.

pH: Hydrogen-ion concentration; reflects how acidic or basic a substance is.

pharynx: The throat; a muscular tube that connects the mouth to the esophagus.

soft palate: The section of the roof of the mouth made of muscle arranged in an arch.

toxic: Poisonous.

voluntary: Acting of one's own free will; by choice.

FOR FURTHER READING

Books

Marion Bennion, *Introduction to Foods.* Englewood Cliffs, NJ: Merill, 1990. Offers good explanations of how foods provide the nutrients essential for human life.

Elizabeth Fong, *Body Structures and Functions.* St. Louis, MO: Times Mirror/Mosby, 1987. Provides simple and thorough descriptions of various diseases of the human body.

Alma Guinness, *ABC's of the Human Body.* Pleasantville, NY: Reader's Digest Association, 1987. Discusses the various structures of the human body and addresses some interesting reasons for certain body functions.

The Handy Science Answer Book. Canton, MI: Visible Ink Press, 1997. Gives very cute explanations for a variety of happenings in the science world.

How in the World? Pleasantville, NY: Reader's Digest Association, 1990. This book provides interesting coverage of both physical and biological events that occur in life.

David E. Larson, *Mayo Clinic Family Health Book.* New York: William Morrow, 1996. Describes in simple terms the many diseases that can affect the human body.

Susan McKeever, *The Dorling Kindersley Science Encyclopedia.* New York: Dorling Kindersley, 1994. Gives concise information on physical and biological occurrences. Good illustrations help explain topics.

Kay Mehas and Sharon Rodgers, *Food Science and You.* New York: Glenco, 1994. This easy-to-read textbook provides nutritional information on food as well as explanations about the human digestive process.

Mary Lou Mulvihill, *Human Diseases.* Norwalk, CT: Appleton & Lange, 1995. This manual on human diseases provides plenty of information on symptoms and treatments.

Nutrition Almanac. New York: McGraw-Hill, 1990. Provides information on the nutritional values of various foods.

Websites

Discovery Channel Website (www.discoveryschool.com) By selecting science topics, students can locate information about topics such as the human digestive tract.

How Stuff Works (www.howstuffworks.com) This website maintained by Marshall Brain has a search engine. By typing in "digestive system," students can access information on how the digestive system works and unusual digestive occurrences. Also provides links to other very informative sites on digestion.

Inner Learning Online (www.innerbody.com) This is an entertaining and informative site on human anatomy that contains animation, graphics, and links to other sites about the human body.

The Yuckiest Site on the Internet (www.yucky.kids.discovery.com) This site has information about the digestive system and some of its quirks.

WORKS CONSULTED

Books

Regina Avraham, *The Digestive System: The Encyclopedia of Health.* New York: Chelsea House, 1989. Describes the structure and function of major and accessory organs in the human digestive system.

Robert Berkow, *The Merck Manual of Medical Information.* New York: Pocket Books, 1997. Provides a detailed explanation of all human digestive organs. This book also gives information on the causes, symptoms, diagnosis, and treatment of many digestive diseases.

Charlotte Dienhart, *Basic Human Anatomy and Physiology.* Philadelphia: W.B. Saunders, 1979. This textbook covers the structure and function of all organ systems in the human body. It also provides information on symptoms and treatments of various diseases.

William C. Goldberg, *Clinical Physiology Made Ridiculously Simple.* Miami, FL: Med Masters, 1995. This booklet gives a very detailed explanation of the functions of all organs in the digestive system. Illustrations reinforce the written content.

John Hole Jr., *Essentials of Human Anatomy and Physiology.* Dubuque, IA: Wm. C. Brown, 1992. This textbook of anatomy and physiology provides detailed explanations of the structure and function of all human digestive organs.

Anthony L. Komaroff, *Harvard Medical School Family Health Guide.* New York: Simon & Schuster, 1999. This book provides comprehensive coverage of the various disorders and diseases that can affect the human body, including symptoms, causes, diagnosis, and treatment options.

Ann Kramer, *The Human Body: The World Book Encyclopedia of Science.* Chicago: World Book, 1987. Provides information on all body systems as well as explanations about unusual and interesting events that occur in the human body.

Stanley Loeb, *The Illustrated Guide to Diagnostic Tests.* Springhouse, PA: Springhouse, 1994. This medical book gives a very thorough explanation of how and why medical technologies are employed to diagnose and treat human diseases and disorders.

Elaine Marieb, *Human Anatomy and Physiology.* Redwood, CA: Benjamin/Cummings, 1995. Offers a very detailed explanation of all human body structures and organs.

Alvin Silverstein, *The Digestive System.* Englewood Cliffs, NJ: Prentice-Hall, 1970. Provides a concise overview of the structure and organs of the digestive system.

Eleanor Noss Whiteney and Sharon Rady Rolfes, *Understanding Nutrition.* Minneapolis, MN: West Publishing, 1993. Gives good information on foods and the nutrients they provide for the human body. Also discusses the importance of nutrients in digestion.

Websites

Leeds University Website (www.leeds.ac.uk) Under health information, this website provided by Leeds University has a comprehensive lecture on the anatomy of the digestive system.

National Digestive Disease Information Clearinghouse (www.niddk.nih.gov). This website provides information on how the human digestive system works. It discusses all digestive processes and how the organs interact to complete digestion.

INDEX

PICTURE CREDITS

ABOUT THE AUTHOR

Pam Walker has sixteen years of experience teaching science in grades seven through twelve. Elaine Wood has taught science for fifteen years in grades seven through twelve. Ms. Walker and Ms. Wood are coauthors of more than a dozen science-teacher resource activity books and two science textbooks.